PRAISE FOR *CREA*
AUTHENTIC ORGAI

CW00408990

'A thought-provoking read from Ryde and Sofianos and a voice of sanity in the asylum; stop what you're doing, read this, and reflect on what you've just stopped doing and where you are going.' **Professor Keith Grint, Professor of Public Leadership & Management, Warwick Business School**

'Forget the so-called balance – work/life has fallen prey to a major M&A. Fittingly, and with savvy timing, Ryde and Sofianos have unmasked authenticity as the critical link to worker survival and organizational sustainability. Based on a seemingly simple premise, the power of the authenticity model is its profound resonance for us all; Worker, Manager, Team Leader, Senior Executive, right through to Board Director. The internal war we battle between our private lives and working world can finally call a truce, with the path to both victory and freedom found in the core message of authenticity championed by Ryde and Sofianos.' **Virginia Haussegger AM, ABC News Anchor, Australia and Adjunct Professor, Institute for Governance and Policy Analysis, University of Canberra**

'19th and 20th century management processes and practices don't work in the knowledge economy of the 21st century. In *Creating Authentic Organizations*, Robin Ryde and Lisa Sofianos thoughtfully and thoroughly frame the rights and responsibilities required to make organizations and individuals successful for today and tomorrow.' **Kai Peters, Chief Executive, Ashridge Business School**

'*Creating Authentic Organizations* is a must-read for any HR professional. The authors emphasize bringing meaning and engagement into the workplace; in essence, making more resilient organizations for the future. More than ever we need to create and sustain resilience in our workplaces; this book provides some very useful ideas, diagnostics and approaches.' **Professor Sir Cary Cooper, Pro-Vice-Chancellor for External Affairs, Lancaster University, and Distinguished Professor of Organizational Psychology and Health, Lancaster University Management School**

'It is refreshing to find a book that explains why the best way to run a business is to be yourself, respect your people and trust everyone with the freedom to do their job in their own way and in their own space. *Creating Authentic Organizations* shows that good management can't be achieved simply by following a process. Success is produced by leaders with character who create a company with personality which is at ease with itself because they pick a group of talented people who 'get it' and trust the organization to trust them to do their best. Managers who take note of the central messages in this book will enjoy a happier and more successful workplace.' **John Timpson, Chairman, Timpson Ltd**

Creating Authentic Organizations

Bringing meaning and engagement back to work

Robin Ryde and
Lisa Sofianos

KoganPage

LONDON PHILADELPHIA NEW DELHI

First published in Great Britain and the United States in 2014 by Kogan Page Limited

2nd Floor, 45 Gee Street	1518 Walnut Street, Suite 1100	4737/23 Ansari Road
London EC1V 3RS	Philadelphia PA 19102	Daryaganj
United Kingdom	USA	New Delhi 110002
		India

www.koganpage.com

ISBN   978 0 7494 7143 9
E-ISBN 978 0 7494 7144 6

British Library Cataloguing-in-Publication Data

A CIP record for this book is available from the British Library.

Library of Congress Cataloging-in-Publication Data

Ryde, Robin.
    Creating authentic organizations : bringing meaning and engagement back to work / Robin Ryde, Lisa Sofianos.
        pages cm
    ISBN 978-0-7494-7143-9 (paperback) — ISBN 978-0-7494-7144-6 (ebook)
1. Employee motivation. 2. Employees—Attitudes. 3. Organizational behavior.
4. Communication in management. 5. Corporate culture. I. Sofianos, Lisa. II. Title.
    HF5549.5.M63R933 2014
    302.3'5—dc23

                                                                                    2014026469

Typeset by Amnet
Print production managed by Jellyfish
Printed and bound by CPI Group (UK) Ltd, Croydon, CR0 4YY

CONTENTS

CREATING AUTHENTIC ORGANIZATIONS

"It is right and necessary that all men should have work to do which shall be worth doing, and be of itself pleasant to do; and which should be done under such conditions as would make it neither over-wearisome nor over-anxious.

WILLIAM MORRIS

"At the most fundamental level of life itself, there is no separation between ourselves and the environment... everything around us, including work and family relationships, is the reflection of our inner lives. Everything is perceived through the self and alters according to the individual's inner state of life.

Thus, if we change ourselves, our circumstances will inevitably change also.

BUDDHIST DOCTRINE OF ONENESS
OF SELF AND ENVIRONMENT

PREFACE

We start this book by wanting to stand back a little from work, and to remember that when we were young we all had ideas, no matter how vague or far-fetched, about what we wanted to do when we grew up. Even though it is mildly ridiculous that having spent only a few years on the earth that anyone would have a realistic idea of what they might do, the very question itself, underlines the significance of work.

The question is one that is asked of children at some point by every parent and every teacher. We have asked it of ourselves too. And the phrasing of the question is worth looking at: 'what do you want to do?' is perhaps the more practical articulation of the thought, but very often the question is 'what do you want to *be* when you grow up?' This suggests something quite fundamental and personal. Being, in these terms, is seen as synonymous with doing. In a broader sense, and perhaps borrowing an existential perspective, that might be the case. But, the being that is referred to here is entirely in the frame of the job or career that we might pursue. No matter how much we might seek to resist the idea that what we do for a job represents who we are as a person, it is hard to argue that they aren't related, at least for many of us. Our self-identity, our value, our contribution, and our hopes are often tied up with work. You only have to look to people who have been unable to find employment, or have remained unemployed for extended periods, to see the effects of this on their sense of self-worth and value.

So we want to start at the beginning in a sense. And we want to start with the voices of people that we interviewed for this book; to hear what imaginings they had when they were young. We don't hold with the idea that work is equal to *being*. Our being, and who we are, is much greater, richer and more varied than work. But contained in the quotations that follow are fragments of the hopes we once had, and a sense of the relatedness between doing and being:

> [When I was growing up] I wanted to be Batgirl, a Solid Gold dancer (like Pan's People), a rock star, and an A&R person. I guess I kind of ended up doing the last thing, in a way, but not in the way that I first envisioned it.

> I wanted to be an actor or barrister. Not dissimilar to being a trainer/facilitator in front of an audience, whom you need to persuade, influence, entertain or

inform. You still need to know your brief/lines, but also be able to engage with, challenge and respond to your audience.

I wanted to do advertising. It's not as exciting as I thought it was going to be – nor is it as glamorous as it is on *Madmen*. But it *is* better than the alternative, which was sticking my arm up cow's fannies, like James Herriot.

I'm a nanny now. I fell into this job as I did with all my jobs since I left school. I stay in this sector as for me it's safe and I'm good at what I do and I do, to a point, enjoy my job. Was it my dream? No. I wanted to be a writer and a social activist, but it turns out I'm not very articulate and lack passion so that's that.

I wanted to be a pirate princess – very sad when I was told that there weren't any in 1970s Cardiff. Now I'm an executive coach and run an organizational change consultancy. There is still a buccaneering element to running my own business and I am my own boss, but I think what I craved as a child was the freedom of being an outsider with no responsibility, and at the moment as a mortgage holder and parent that's a tough call.

I was 100 per cent focused on joining the police force, which I did for a short while, followed by working in the City and finally working in education. Compared to what I do now, it couldn't be further apart. My work now is much more satisfying, less complicated and I can guide my business in the direction which suits me.

I wanted to be in the performing arts industry. My job role is not comparable as I am in the IT training and consultancy industry which is great as I have a love of IT and I enjoy meeting new people at different levels and travelling.

I wanted to be a soldier. But as I grew up I realized that I didn't really want to kill people, be shouted at, or wear a uniform. I now work in an Audit Office. WTF!

I wanted to write commercials, be a chef or run a hotel when I was wee. I did used to work in advertising but that was soul destroying after the novelty wore off. What I do now has evolved from the choices I've made along the way. I didn't actively seek out this position but now I look up and two years have gone by.

I didn't foresee myself doing anything at all. My father was a priest and I didn't have the calling for it… Nowadays I am s'posed to be a graphic designer but I don't know how much longer that will hold true, I mean, how many 50-year-old graphic designers have you fed popcorn to recently? If you'd asked me at another time in my life I could have equally said 'I'm a runner in a bigass media corporation' or 'I'm a receptionist in a shitty zero-star hotel' and they would both have been transiently true.

I wanted to be a vet when I was younger, but from an early age I decided that I wasn't capable of getting the grades I would need so abandoned the idea. My older self knows it would have been achievable. I am now a retail buyer, my childhood hopes and dreams in tatters, my life an endless and pointless circle of drivel.

I wanted to be an author. I think its only because in school once I got an A in English for an essay I wrote which made me feel I could do something well. Everything I did before then I got a C or worse. Its strange really, this business of imagining what you might be when you get old. I think I just wanted to do something important. I feel like I'm on my way there but it may take until my next lifetime to get there.

I always wanted to be a paediatrician. I can very distinctly remember being at the Royal Children's Hospital at 9 years old, when my sister was in hospital and I told myself that one day, I wanted to work there. And I did. And even though now I work in a more population health focused paediatric role, I still see myself as a paediatrician first and foremost and a member of the Royal Children's Hospital, which I still am, as I still work there part time. I feel more at home at the Hospital than I do at [my organisation] and feel it is my professional home.

I wanted to work in the Music industry, which I did for a while before becoming totally disillusioned with it. What I do now feels far more creative, and more importantly for me is that the success of it isn't performance related or dependent on market forces.

I wanted to be a writer. Writing is central to my job (although I'm not a best-selling author!), so I kind of achieved my goal.

I wanted to be a film cameraman (films not television) but missed the application deadline by a day for a British Film Foundation apprenticeship. I now shovel heaps of cash from one pile to another for a fund management company.

I always wanted to be a teacher from an early age, I loved it and still like to help Rich, my husband [who is now a teacher], with his planning.

ACKNOWLEDGEMENTS

This book was written by two people but inspired and supported by very many more.

We would like to give our thanks to both Timpson and Karmarama, two of the case study organizations for this work. In particular we'd like to thank John and James Timpson and also Jay Housden who spent a considerable amount of his time introducing us to Timpson colleagues and letting use loose around a variety of Timpson stores. We thank Ben Bilboul, Dave Buonaguidi and other colleagues of Karmarama for inviting us into their organization and speaking so openly with us.

We are very lucky to have been able to rely on numerous people from different work backgrounds, and from across the globe, who have contributed to the book by testing emerging ideas, offering their insights in the research phase and being the best possible sounding boards. These include Sarah Allen, Neil Barns, Michelle Bayes, Richard Bell, Henry Broughton, Rich Cannon, Robert Chatwin, Jane Durlacher, Tricia Donnelly, Mark Edmonson, Sophie Everett, Angie Flange, Roger Flopple, Fiona Forrest, Phil Greenfluff, Jane Hatcher, Cheryl McGee, Elliot Lord, Dr Milk, Fiona Manklow, Mark Nelson, Jenny Proimos, Allison Schnackenberg, Bill Schaper, Ivor Semion, Belinda Shurlin, Jackie St Angela Stone, Dominic Thackray, Marilyn Tyler, Charlie Waterhouse, Shirley Wong, Danny Willis and Tom York. Thank you to Leon Sofianos, and to Stella and Les Ryde for always being available to help out.

We would like to dedicate this book to Jackson and Frankie Ryde in the hope that whatever work they find themselves doing in later life it is enjoyable, meaningful and worthwhile.

The building blocks of authenticity
A summary for busy people

> *This above all,*
> *To thine own self be true,*
> *And it must follow, as the night the day,*
> *Thou canst not then be false to any man.*
>
> **POLONIUS IN *HAMLET*, ACT I, SCENE III, WILLIAM SHAKESPEARE**

> *Be exactly who you want to be, do what you want to do*
> *I am he and she is she but, you're the only you*
> *No one else has got your eyes, can see the things you see*
> *It's up to you to change your life, and my life's up to me*
> *The problems that you suffer from are problems that*
>   *you make*
> *The shit we have to climb through is the shit we choose*
>   *to take*
> *If you don't like the life you live, change it now it's yours*
> *Nothing has effects if you don't recognise the cause*
> *If the programme's not the one you want, get up, turn off*
>   *the set*
> *It's only you who can decide what life you're gonna get.*
>
> **PENNY RIMBAUD, CRASS, 'BIG A LITTLE A'**

Work and authenticity matters

Authenticity, until now perhaps, has rarely been thought of as a major driver of organizational performance. We do not usually think of authenticity as a key competitive advantage, a value-creating factor or an adaptive mechanism. In fact, perhaps with the exception of its narrow application in recent years to leadership, authenticity has been largely omitted from the landscape of organizational thinking. However, we are in no doubt that these descriptions are right and that in years to come authenticity will be understood as a key variable that separates successful from failing businesses, happy from disengaged workforces, and adaptive from inflexible organizations. Authenticity delivers a benefit to employees and to organizations alike, and in doing so, benefits then fall to customers and stakeholders also. Authenticity offers what might be described in economic terms as a multiplier effect, and it is for these and other reasons, that authenticity is a valuable personal and organizational asset, and one worth creating.

With this in mind, we start with two fundamental questions: what does it mean to be authentic at work, and why might this matter?

Definitions of authenticity vary but a useful anchoring definition is to think of authenticity as the degree to which one is true to one's own personality, spirit or character, despite external pressures. The shadow of external pressures described here is an important part of the definition, as it alludes to a tension between who we are and how we might then be able to express this in the world. Furthermore, if we take for example the notion that 'one is true to one's own personality' we must also entertain the thought that firstly one has to come to understand one's own personality, and secondly, that the personality is subject to change. With this in mind it is helpful to draw on a more dynamic interpretation so that we might see authentic people engaging in processes of:

- discovering who they are;
- imagining what they might be;
- divining meaning in what they do;
- finding their own terms of self-expression; and
- breaking out of the externally imposed expectations referred to.

Moving our attention to the world of work, where people may or may not be able to find their authenticity, it helps to recognize how significant work is in our lives. Most people, that is, over 4 billion people, spend most of their waking hours in work. And furthermore, most of our adult years see us engaged in paid and non-paid labour. Much of our mental energy, our ideas, our passions, our physical effort and our time is deployed in work. Many of us in fact meet our future spouses while at work. Many establish life-long friendships with colleagues, and many cite the workplace as a major source of learning and growth. Our identity is often bound up in what we do at work. The work we do goes some way to describing who we are, what we stand for and it reveals, in one dimension at least, a tangible and valued contribution that we make to the world. Authenticity and work matter.

The shifting shape of work

Over the last few hundred years the shape of work has changed dramatically and this is important context. For the majority of people, until recent times, work has been a largely physical endeavour requiring us to either make or grow our means for survival or to sell our physical labour for a wage. We call this the era of 'Work in the Hand'. One of the biggest changes for workers during this time was precipitated by the Industrial Revolution of the late 1700s with the shift in the location of work from the home or surrounding land, to factories that contained machinery capable of mass production. Work became a place that one travelled to which was set apart from the home and community context – a dislocation that was intensified by the huge influxes of people from the countryside to factories in the rapidly growing towns and cities. We got organized around work. The business of work became more repetitive and mechanized and manufacturers, in order to maximize profit, developed workplace cultures that focused on standardization, streamlining and economy. As a consequence of the large scale of many organizations and the pursuit of efficiency, there was a move towards tightly managed procedures in order to govern the behaviour of individuals. This has shaped our workplaces for centuries and has resulted in a set of norms and values that are quite distinct from those to be found in personal life.

We are now moving into an era that we call 'Work in the Head', associated most recently with the Knowledge Economy, where thought, individuality, creativity and expertise are valuable commodities. And in this context, employers hope to access the experiences, beliefs and processes that belong to the individual in search of competitive advantage, making ever greater inroads into territories that were once entirely private. Table 1.1 illustrates this shift.

TABLE 1.1 How the requirements of Work in the Head differ from Work in the Hand

Work in the Hand	Work in the Head
Restricted to specific locations	Always with us, not dependent upon location
Standardized (templates, systems, models)	Constantly changing and adapting to shifting circumstances
Focus on activity and filling every moment with production	Focus on mental effort, invention, possibilities and sense making
Minimization of mental distraction and 'time-wasting'	Personal investment using life experiences as material
Simplicity, reproducibility and efficiency	Embracing complexity and valuing individuality
Means of production owned by employers	Means of production owned by workers

The division of the self

With this, we have seen how work and home life have become separated over the centuries into two domains, with their own distinct cultures. Our industrialized past has created the conditions for what might be thought of as a 'schism' between how people are expected to be at work, and how they can act outside of work. This schism we have taken with us into the era of Work in the Head and along with it a set of tools, assumptions and mind sets that are not fully adapted to current requirements.

In the modern context when we go to work, we continue to discard our private selves and don our work personas in the process of conforming to the norms of the workplace. Somewhere along our journey to work, we make changes and adjustments to our language, demeanour, sense of identity and appearance, as a host of assumptions and customs begin to act upon us. The sense of the divide between paid work and our private lives is no more keenly felt than during the process of remaking ourselves in preparation for entering into work. Most people, for example, will wear formal office attire for a job interview or when meeting a corporate client for the first time. The semiotic value of a suit and tie cannot be underestimated, and carries within it the whole philosophy of our industrialized past. It describes ideas of uniformity and standardization, efficiency, minimization of distracting choices and reproducibility.

We know that the two worlds are interwoven, but we find our personality being divided into two factions. We are estranged and strangers to ourselves; having to construct ourselves in each domain as if the other doesn't exist. Speaking to one of our interviewees for this book we were told a story that illustrates this well. The interviewee – a professional, high-earning woman who also had young children – described how, on a number of occasions, she had unexpectedly been forced to work from home to cover for child care problems. While on the phone to both clients and colleagues, with her children making noises in the background (as they do), she would make up stories so that the person on the other end of the call wouldn't think she was working from home – 'Oh, forgive the background noise I'm just walking past a school' she would say, or 'Let me just shut the door to my office, its like a zoo out there'. At work we shut out the non-work self and vice versa.

One of the many consequences of this duality in the workplace is stress, which is shouldered at the level of the individual and the organization. The Labour Force Survey for 2011 to 2012 revealed that 10.4 million working days were lost to stress-related illness in the UK.[1] The World Health Organization cites work-related stress as an issue of growing concern in developing countries 'due to processes of globalization and the changing nature of work'.[2] The search for 'work–life balance' has been an earnest and well-intentioned attempt to tackle this schism, but still it nevertheless seeks to treat work and non-work as separate domains – hopefully in slightly better balance. And it is perhaps no surprise then that as technological advances enable employers to increasingly encroach on private life, that people feel that they have failed.

The value of authenticity

At the personal level we believe that authenticity is the missing piece in this puzzle and a means by which these two falsely divided worlds can be reunited. By being authentic across both domains we are able to recognize who we really are, without capitulating to a need to suppress important values, without wearing a mask to make us more palatable to others, and without experiencing the loss of engagement or drive that so often goes with presenting an emaciated version of ourselves. A friend of ours[3] jokingly suggested that in keeping with the workplace tradition of 'bring your child to work' or 'bring your pet to work' day, that there might be a 'bring yourself to work' day. Think about it. It makes you giggle, but the point here is a serious one. Wouldn't it be better to bring the whole you to work, but not just one day in the year, but every day? There are some limits to this for sure, but far fewer than we might think.

Apart from the work that authenticity does to solve the schism of the self, we also believe at the individual level that greater authenticity is the key to a treasure chest of other benefits. Authentic people are able to benefit from:

- high levels of motivation – which are directly related to the opportunity to meaningfully apply one's own thoughts and experience to the task in hand;
- greater levels of engagement with the numerous attendant benefits – well-being, productivity, commitment and so on;
- greater pride in the work done – as employees are allowed to craft their own solutions, they are able to take greater pride in the results that they have created;
- the ability to leverage one's own particular strengths to the job;
- being able to express and be yourself, without having to pretend to be something you are not; and
- much greater learning through a deeper search for meaning and personal application.

The prize that is offered to the individual employee is significant in its own right, and if that were where the story ended, then this would still be worth fighting for. But we also believe that if this is done right then the organizations that we work for stand to benefit enormously from:

- Greater resourcefulness and innovation – as workers seek to source solutions to their own issues and feel able to freely explore a greater range of possibilities, their resourcefulness, creativity and innovation increases. Not only does this deliver a benefit to the task but it also raises capability across, and for, the organization.
- Employees having more 'skin in the game' and therefore more commitment to the success of the organization – too often employees

find themselves in the 'consent and evade' space where they may ostensibly accept corporate messages and initiatives but in practice do not truly feel responsible for them. Authenticity inspires workers to commit in ways that breeds engagement and greater interest in the organization's success.

- Greater accountability and ownership in the workplace – as employees find ways to express themselves in their work, and engage more fully in their work, they also build a greater sense of ownership about what they and others do in the workplace. And as workers feel more responsible for the results they create, so do they feel more accountable for the product of their efforts.

- Agility and adaptability in the face of changing circumstances – highly motivated and engaged employees continually look for options to improve their work, and because they may be located close to the 'coal face', they are able to detect and respond to changes in the environment such as shifts in customer expectations. They are also better equipped to see and act upon opportunities and will rightly feel empowered to act.

- High productivity – we know from the work of Daniel Pink and David McClelland that autonomy and the opportunity to make an impact is a key driver of productivity.

The greatest driver of authenticity: The Freedoms and Authenticity model

The question that follows from this is what needs to happen for people to be more authentic at work? We offer in this book a means of addressing just this. The offer is made to people at all levels in the organization, and is not a model just for the 'workers', or the management, or the leadership, rather this carries equal weight wherever you sit in the organization. The Freedoms and Authenticity model encapsulates this strategy for pursuing authenticity and it comprises three overlapping areas, or 'freedoms'. These are shown in Table 1.2.

Our recommendation is, in conjunction with the diagnostic tool in Chapter 7, that you build a sense of how you compare to each of the three freedoms and explore the scope for you to extend your reach in relation to each freedom. Following these steps will greatly enhance the level of authenticity you are able to demonstrate at work.

TABLE 1.2 The Freedoms and Authenticity Model

The Freedom to Operate (F2O)	The freedom to arrange your affairs in the way you think best to accomplish your goals.
The Freedom to Speak (F2S)	The freedom to offer your views in a way which isn't censored or constrained by others, in particular by those at higher levels in the hierarchy.
The Freedom to Actualize (F2A)	The freedom to assume and realize an identity and perspective that is different from others' and reflects your own emergent personality and values.

However, the responsibility for claiming authenticity and for exercising the three freedoms must ultimately rest with the individual. Our philosophical perspective, to the extent that we offer one, has shades of Libertarianism. We see people as self-governing individuals who make choices and are responsible for them. Authenticity is rightly a concern for all, but it is for the individual to define it for themselves, to strive to attain it (should they choose to), and importantly to resist giving way to the temptation that it is the job of management to furnish it for them. My authenticity sits with me, yours with you, and it is not our belief that it is anyone's responsibility to find it or 'fix it' for someone else.

Importantly, as workers claim these freedoms they also face associated obligations, for example the obligation to become informed about corporate priorities to ensure a fit with the enactment of the Freedom to Operate, and the obligation to learn from the exercise of freedoms and to share this more broadly.

The Freedom to Operate

The Freedom to Operate (F2O) identified in the Freedoms Model involves allowing employees to reach their own judgements on the best strategies for fulfilling the tasks they face, and being allowed to execute on this basis. The question of how the work should be tackled is one that rests firmly with the employee. But more than this, even when it comes to alternative conceptualizations about what the task itself should entail, this too should be in the domain of control of the individual.

Employees are both invited and trusted to be creative in the way they shape and deliver their work. Under this model, the freedoms that they might claim in relation to this could be manifest in a range of ways. For example, some workers may make particular judgements about the timing and pacing of activities in their portfolio. Others may want to form particular partnerships or collaborations in order to accomplish their work. Judgements might be made about the best style or modus operandi to employ to achieve the results required. Some workers may choose to deploy technology in support of their aims or alternatively select face-to-face communications as their primary strategy. All of these choices are available to, and in the gift of, the workers to whom the tasks belong.

There are understandable limits to what is possible in that organizations have a different Absolute Freedom to Operate (AF2O) based on their industry, and individual roles reflect a different Residual Freedom to Operate (RF2O). For example, a nuclear power plant might be thought of as conferring a narrow Absolute Freedom to Operate, while the role of public relations manager within it, might possess a wide Residual Freedom to Operate. So these 'realities' need to be understood, but our encouragement is to creatively challenge these limitations to loosen-up opportunities to exercise the Freedom to Operate.

Our case study of Timpson[4] (see p 62) illustrates this well with workers being explicitly afforded the Freedom to Operate. This is signalled in a number of ways that include the convention that in every store in the country there will be a large sign on the wall picturing the company's Chairman John Timpson and the message: 'You have my authority to do whatever you think will best give an amazing service.' This is a message directed at workers and underscores the company's ethos and its attitude to staff empowerment and authenticity.

The Freedom to Speak

In a modern operating context that is characterized by volatility, uncertainty, complexity and ambiguity, the sense making function of an organization is remarkably valuable. The task needs to belong not only to the leaders but people at every layer and every discipline in the organization. The importance of this persistent and unfettered enquiry is articulated well by David Cooperrider: 'Human systems grow in the direction of what they persistently ask questions about.'[5]

The Freedom to Speak (F2S) identified as the second element to the Freedoms Model carries a more expansive meaning than it might appear on first reading. While this is about the importance of employees being able to articulate their ideas, feelings, hopes and concerns within the organization, and doing so without censorship or constraint, it is also a strong encouragement for this to happen – often, and to a deep level. As a consequence of this workers therefore:

- speak freely and often, about their views and ideas (turn up the volume of dialogue);
- talk about their views and ideas in a way that is honest, authentic and at a deep level (raise the quality of dialogue);
- discuss issues relating to the meaning and value of the work they do, and their ability to be authentic in the workplace (leverage the benefits of the personal domain);
- discuss issues relating to organizational well being, particularly where they are picking up data and signs relating to opportunities or threats (leverage the benefits of the organizational domain);
- ensure that important information, ideas and perspectives make the leap from the informal arena into the formal realm;
- make nothing unsayable (within reason) in the formal space. Name and discuss the 'elephant in the room' – it may be the most valuable contribution that can be made.

The Freedom to Actualize

The Freedom to Actualize (F2A) identified as the third element to the Freedoms Model focuses on the freedom to assume and realize an identity and perspective that is different from others' and reflects your own emergent personality and values. But capturing the dynamic quality of this as discussed earlier, it is helpful to frame this in four dimensions which involves work:

- To be – this refers to the extent to which people are able to assume and express their identity and personality at work. This may be manifest in a number of ways ranging from how people dress to the way that individual skills are brought into work.
- To discover – this refers to the opportunity that work allows for people to gain an appreciation of their unique preferences, skills and interests, as well as to discover at a deeper level the meaning of what they do.
- To imagine – this refers to the extent to which work provides a space and the encouragement for people to develop possibilities, explore ideas and to imagine how they might develop and grow.

● To become – this refers to the encouragement, acceptance and facilitation that work offers for people to re-shape their identities and practically realize their potential as individuals (to be applied more broadly than the workplace alone).

The artificial division between the work self and the non-work self is exactly the problem that the Freedom to Actualize is seeking to solve. The schism discussed earlier is real and it is born from the idea that the set of experiences, aspirations, and feelings that relate to our non-work self have little to do with the experiences, aspirations and feelings that we associate with our work self. In this way, to divide them and keep them separate is seen as a logical step to take. But this, of course, doesn't stand up to analysis. The only difference between the two worlds is the purpose to which the same body of experiences, aspirations and feelings[6] are put. And once we recognize this merger between the two worlds, then the case for exploring the person you are, and the person you become in work, is very powerful.

In exploring the Freedom to Actualize we might see ourselves engaging in a rich set of issues including how we can express ourselves at work, what needs to be in place for us to be 'in flow', the judgements we need to make to ensure we act in alignment with our values, the self-awareness we inevitably develop, the search for meaning and purpose in the work we do, our ability to open up and avoid defensiveness with others and so on.

Our case study of the UK Advertising Agency Karmarama[7] (see p 116) provides an excellent insight into the Freedom to Actualize. It draws out the agency's invention of the concept of 'Good Works' which described a desire to move away from the excesses that they feel have characterized the advertising and communications industry as self-serving and perhaps obnoxious in many eyes.

Their commitment to creating an invigorating, playful and enjoyable working environment is legendary. All employees are housed on the same floor within one enormous space to encourage maximum collaboration and cross-fertilization of ideas. Visitors enter Karmarama via a light tunnel that indicates that one should expect the unexpected, and through to a modest reception area that is refreshingly free of awards and then into the canteen where they are pitched into the heart of the agency. Once inside, the space is zoned into relaxation areas, cubby holes, open meeting spaces, traditional groupings of desks, so that people can find the setting that best suits their working need in the moment. Great efforts have been made to reinforce the message that working at Karmarama is stimulating, inclusive and fun. The senior team look indistinguishable from their colleagues and use the work spaces provided for everyone. Large artworks punctuate the office landscape, and expressions of individual creativity and ingenuity are encouraged as part of the daily life of the office. Housed behind the main workspace are a series of table tennis tables used by agency workers and serious athletes alike. There is even a tuck shop and a micro-brewery to set the scene of home-grown fun and innovation. Karmarama's 'no w*****s' policy which can be seen in giant neon lights in reception point to the idea that how people treat one another at work is important and non-negotiable.

The management task

For managers exercising their own authenticity, there are opportunities to lend support to others doing the same. Let us be clear though that the individual rather than the organization, the management or the leadership stands centre stage in the pursuit of authenticity. The manager may make an occasional cameo appearance or may work backstage to put the right conditions in place, but their role is secondary.

With this in mind we make available to managers five priorities and five related roles (Table 1.3): not only does the 5 'A's Management Task support authenticity but the qualities we describe fit much better with a contemporary interpretation of management which departs in important ways from the planning, organizing, monitoring, controlling paradigm that is usually reached for.

TABLE 1.3 The 5 'A's management task of authenticity

	Focus	Management role descriptor
1	Authenticity	Freedoms fighter
2	Adaptation	Head of learning and development
3	Alignment	Interpreter
4	Accountability	Accountability steward
5	Action	Occasional interventionist

These activities are described in detail later in the book but we make three key comments here. Firstly, managers have a key role to play in fighting for the freedoms outlined so far. The power they possess as role models is considerable, but more than this we look to the value that managers can deliver in creating the right environment for authenticity to develop. Much in the same way that an owner of fish might look after a fish tank; cleaning it, feeding the fish, creating an engaging environment, so should the manager in the organizational space. Secondly, there is a need for managers to play a much greater role in sense making, learning and adaptation than ever before. Too many organizations have been caught out in recent years by technological changes, economic contractions, socio-cultural shifts and so on and this is because the tasks of sense making, learning and adaptation have either been left to those at the top of the organizational pyramid, or haven't been undertaken quickly or well enough. The function that managers can play in this regard is invaluable and this suggests that a much greater level of interest in the topic and much greater sophistication is required; whether this is about better understanding about how learning occurs, the contribution of the behavioural sciences, or the relevance of experiments and trials – all invite a new level of mastery.

Thirdly, we see managers as an accountability lynchpin with the organization. Stood, like the Colossus of Rhodes, astride the two headlands of local delivery and corporate leadership, managers can make a unique contribution. We see managers as a force that can hold workers to account for corporate priorities, but also holding the leadership accountable for its obligations. The former of these two accountabilities is usually a routine part of the role, but the latter is less practised. In these times, this dimension of managerial accountability has a great deal to offer.

A final nudge in the right direction

We finish this summary with a familiar story looked at through the lens of authenticity.

There once was a shepherd boy who was bored as he sat on the hillside watching the village sheep. To amuse himself he took a great breath and sang out, 'Wolf! Wolf! The wolf is chasing the sheep!' The villagers came running up the hill to help the boy drive the wolf away. But when they arrived at the top of the hill, they found no wolf. The boy laughed at the sight of their angry faces. 'Don't cry "wolf", shepherd boy,' said the villagers, 'When there's no wolf!' They went grumbling back down the hill.

Later, the boy sang out again, 'Wolf! Wolf! The wolf is chasing the sheep!' To his naughty delight, he watched the villagers run up the hill to help him drive the wolf away. When the villagers saw no wolf they sternly said, 'Save your frightened song for when there is really something wrong! Don't cry "wolf" when there is no wolf!'

But the boy just grinned and watched them go grumbling down the hill once more. Later, he saw a real wolf prowling about his flock. Alarmed, he leapt to his feet and sang out as loudly as he could, 'Wolf! Wolf!' But the villagers thought he was trying to fool them again, and so they didn't come.

At sunset, everyone wondered why the shepherd boy hadn't returned to the village with their sheep. They went up the hill to find the boy. They found him weeping. 'There really was a wolf here! The flock has scattered! I cried out, "Wolf!" Why didn't you come?' The old man attempted to comfort the boy, as his blood boiled within.

There is one winner to this story, and two losers:

- The winner is of course the wolf that got a handsome meal in the process. We might think of the wolf as the competition. Interestingly, the wolf didn't need to change anything about the way it conducted its business, the wolf just carried on as usual and took the advantage that the boy unwittingly provided.

- The first loser is of course the boy, who as an employee is unlikely to be trusted with the role of Shepherd again. His dismissal papers are probably in the post.

- But the second loser is the townspeople (the organization), and all of them, as they collectively relied on the boy in protecting their food supply that now sits in the belly of the competition.

Our moral of this tale is that authenticity between colleagues and across all levels of the system is of first order importance. This is why most of this book is written on the premise that employees and culture come first in constructing authenticity and with it comes the benefits mentioned including trust, responsibility, accountability and engagement – all of which were absent in the tale of the wolf and the boy. With authentic people, we make authentic organizations.

But we recognize that the workforce is not synonymous with the organization. While in terms of a Venn diagram the two circles cross and there is a considerable overlap between the two domains, organizations can possess a power, identity, symbolic value, legal status etc that is different from the individuals that make it up.

TABLE 1.4 Seven additional nudges and tips to be adopted at the organizational level to create authentic organizations

	Additional nudges to achieve authenticity at the organizational level
1	Publicly declare what the organization stands for (and will not stand for).
2	Proactively engage in real, two-way, adult-to-adult dialogue with all that are interested.
3	Turn the organization into a 'glass house' (highly transparent).
4	Humanize the points of interaction between organization and clients, customers, enquirers etc.
5	Follow the organization's influence as far as it goes and assess the impact against its standards.
6	Admit to, and share learning from, mistakes.
7	Don't change the deal (with customers or employees) and expect no one to notice.

We consider therefore what it is that might need to be in place for an organization to be authentic that isn't covered by the authenticity that is created at an individual/workforce level. Most of the important work is already done if employees are our priority, but to maximize the chances of success, we propose seven 'nudges' and tips, explained in greater depth later, which will get any organization beyond the tipping point, as shown in Table 1.4.

In Chapter 2 we start at the beginning of work itself, and dig deeper into why the modern working environment challenges authenticity at every turn.

Notes

1 UK Health and Safety Executive's Stress and Psychological Disorders in Great Britain 2013.

2 Protecting Workers' Health Series No. 6, Raising awareness of stress at work in developing countries, Irene Houtman and Karin Jettinghoff, TNO Work &

Employment, The Netherlands, and Leonor Cedillo, Occupational Health researcher, Mexico © World Health Organization 2007.

3   Thanks to Rosie Stevens.

4   Timpson is a shoe repairing, key cutting, sign making etc company. It has around 1,000 stores in the United Kingdom and employs over 2,500 people.

5   www.sekerkaethicsinaction.com/docs/pdfs/Cooperrider-Sekerka%20 Chapter%20Web%201-06.pdf

6   In this we include a broad range of other qualities such as skills, interests, thinking, values etc.

7   Karmarama is one of the leading creative independent communications agencies in the United Kingdom. The agency was founded in 2000 and, at the time of writing, is 250-people strong and responsible for a raft of successful campaigns for companies such as Costa Coffee, BBC, British Telecom and Honda.

Solomon's solution

02

In order to engage in a discussion about workplace authenticity it is first necessary to put work in context, and an historical one at that. This chapter invites the reader to contemplate what has happened to work over the years and at the same time to consider how this has affected our relationship to work.

We want to start with an exploration of the location of work, and for this we offer two distinct shifts in its history, namely the age of 'Work in the Hand' and the age of 'Work in the Head'. Both of these eras make a difference in terms of their impact on our ability to be authentic. Our proposition is that, as we have moved through these two eras we have been faced with a serious dilemma; one that is similar to that faced by King Solomon. In the tale of King Solomon, two women sought the arbitration of the King while both claiming to be the birth mother of the same child. Unable to determine the child's birth mother amid the protestations of each woman, he proposed that the only way to solve the issue was to cut the baby in two so that each mother might have half. The story continues that the birth mother revealed herself by claiming that she would rather let the child live with the other woman, than see the sword sever her child, while the false mother also revealed herself by remaining quiet.

Our dilemma in work is over the seemingly inevitable division of the self that we face when we accept going to work. Like Solomon we find ourselves faced with an impossible judgement, and an equally unworkable solution, which is to divide our being, our identity, our purpose and our passions between work and non-work.

Work in the Hand

Throughout history, our lives have been characterized by a struggle to survive and a desire to live in the way that we choose. At the centre of this journey has always been work of one sort or another. Even the earliest communities of human beings would spend their days tirelessly searching for food; finding and securing shelter; caring for the young; and protecting themselves from harm as best they could. Life must have been physically exhausting as the principal source of power was our own bodies or those of the animals that we could encourage to work for us. The only way to increase productivity was to increase manpower and the size of a community was a governing factor in its resilience and survival in the face of hardship. Although people were innovating and inventing throughout this time, the vast majority of work was physical and we will be referring throughout this chapter to this kind of activity as 'Work in the Hand'.

As is the way of humans, we got better at this kind of work, inventing tools and equipment to overcome our physical limitations. They were such a great success that, over time, and through a huge investment in technology, we industrialized these processes, creating greater volume of goods and more income generation. Now, one human being could manufacture vast quantities of the things we needed in comparison to the pre-industrial era. People were still needed to work alongside machines in a physical capacity in order to operate the machinery and to complete the more delicate tasks. And so the era of Work in the Hand extended throughout the Industrial Revolution to the 20th century.

Travelling to work

One of the biggest changes for workers during the Industrial Revolution was the shift in the location of their work from the home or surrounding land, where agricultural or cottage industries such as spinning and weaving took place, to factories filled with the machinery of mass production. Workers no longer lived alongside their workplaces as large and expensive specialized equipment that was financially beyond the reach of ordinary people, came to be essential to production on an industrial scale. Work became a place that one travelled to which was set apart from the home and community context, and this dislocation was intensified by the huge influxes of people from the countryside to factories in the rapidly growing towns and cities.

Marx famously observed that the majority of working people no longer owned their 'means of production' – the looms, forges and land that they had previously employed to make goods that they could choose to use, stockpile or sell as a return on their labour. Instead, the entire product of their labour was given to their employer in exchange for a wage. Without the means to manufacture according to their needs, workers were rendered dependent upon their employer for both money and goods. Marx observed that, as workers became less able to exert control over their lives and more separated from the results of their labour, a type of alienation occurred:

> Two centuries ago, our forebears would have known the precise history and origin of nearly every one of the limited number of things that they ate and owned, as well as of the people and tools involved in their production. They were acquainted with the pig, the carpenter, the weaver, the loom and the dairymaid. The range of items available for purchase may have grown exponentially since then, but our understanding of their genesis has diminished almost to the point of obscurity. We are now as imaginatively disconnected from the manufacture and distribution of our goods as we are practically in reach of them, a process of alienation which has stripped us of myriad opportunities for wonder, gratitude and guilt.[1]

Workers who had relocated from their rural settings became shorn of their community context and estranged from their own human experience through working in an increasingly mechanized fashion. They became de-skilled as a consequence, abandoning traditionally skill and craft-led occupations, which in turn increased their dependence upon employers for a wage. The resulting power asymmetry between workers and employers created the conditions for employers to dictate the terms on which their employees engaged with their work. This legacy is still with us and can be seen in the readiness with which people choose to put the demands of their employer, before their own.

Mass production, productivity and being fined for whistling on the job

To give an idea of the speed at which industrialization transformed the world of work, it is helpful to look to 19th-century Britain, and the examples of Richard Arkwright, believed to be the architect of the factory model, and Edmund Cartwright. In 1769 Arkwright patented the 'Water Frame', a mechanized spinning frame, and shortly after created the first true factory in Cromford, near Derby:

> This act was to change Great Britain. Before very long, this factory employed over 300 people. Nothing had ever been seen like this before. The domestic system only needed two to three people working in their own home. By 1789, the Cromford mill employed 800 people. With the exception of a few engineers in the factory, the bulk of the workforce were essentially unskilled. They had their own job to do over a set number of hours. Whereas those in the domestic

system could work their own hours and enjoyed a degree of flexibility, those in the factories were governed by a clock and factory rules. Edmund Cartwright's power loom ended the life style of skilled weavers. In the 1790's, weavers were well paid. Within 30 years many had become labourers in factories as their skill had now been taken over by machines. In 1813, there were only 2,400 power looms in Britain. By 1850, there were 250,000.[2]

Factories are, of course, run for profit and from the outset strict rules were formulated around limiting any kind of distracting behaviour in an effort to direct all activity towards the service of production. Arkwright imposed fines for seemingly the most trivial of actions such as whistling on the factory floor. Any activity that impacted on profit was restricted, including safeguarding the workers from injury.

Getting serious about efficiency

Moving into the 20th century, conditions had greatly improved for workers; however the demand for efficiency and the minimization of activity that could reduce production and profit necessarily remained. Waste/inefficiency reducing systems extended to the daily life of the workers within factories, where huge efforts were made to streamline production through fragmenting activity into repetitive and specialized processes. In this way the Ford Motor Company moved from the inefficient model of employing teams of skilled workers to assemble cars from available components produced by outside suppliers, to one where Ford-manufactured parts were assembled by unskilled workers following a series of simple and repetitive actions. Workers were not even required to move from their station as their work came to them on the automated assembly line. We are all aware of how these innovations drove incredible success for Ford.

This system-driven thinking has persisted into the 21st century and has been perfected since Ford's vision of workers as an extension of machine parts through models such as Lean and Six Sigma. Toyota's production system seeks to incorporate potential for human ingenuity, something that they found lacking in the Ford System, by requiring workers to act in a quality control capacity. However, a common thread throughout all of these innovations is the idea that activity that does not drive profit and distracts from the physical process of production is to be designed out of the system.

This is the historical context that has moulded the modern workplace, its norms, values and expectations. It is a place where we feel dependent upon our employer for the means to create financial security. In a world where many of us have general skills with little to differentiate what we can offer, the competition for each job is high, so we must demonstrate our loyalty by placing the demands of the workplace before our own. In an endless drive towards efficiency we speak in a limited vocabulary that orients us away from the personal. In fact, in some corporate environments it might be hard to imagine that the people sat behind the desks have real and vibrant lives outside of the office. We eliminate individuality at every turn in our effort to focus all of our attention upon our paid work.

All change

This brief account of a slice of work history has led us to where we are now. However, and inevitably, the world of work is in another period of rapid change, arguably on a par with that of the Industrial Revolution.

The factors acting upon businesses, workplaces and individuals at this moment, such as the impact of fast-moving technological advances, require another shift in perception about how we work. Individuals, in their capacity as workers and consumers, are more interconnected, better informed, and ready to challenge the current wisdom than ever before. Likewise, businesses and organizations are desperately making sense of the consequences of issues such as changing demographics and global markets, to their own operations.

The Industrial Model of work was forged in a long period of relative stability and in an era of deference. And we believe that it is no longer serving us and a new model is required. This new model contains two key elements that are central to the next phase of our evolution, namely the need to withstand and harness the dynamics of change and complexity, and to accommodate the need for self-determinism within individuals.

Globalization has seen the fortunes of businesses and organizations tied to events occurring on the other side of the world, as the global financial crisis has revealed. Banking institutions are interwoven in a complex tapestry of financial arrangements that means when one falls as a result of poor decision-making, the rest are catastrophically impacted along with governments, pensioners, public sector workers and ultimately whole nations. Technology have made, and continues to remake, the way we interact with each other unrecognizable compared with recent history. In just a few decades we have become accustomed to talking to a world without geographical barriers via text and e-mail and social media. Almost no one is inaccessible and every viewpoint can potentially find an audience. The internet has brought us a river of information that can be accessed from our phones. Generations of young people cannot conceive of a time when this connectedness with the rest of the world was not possible. They live in a world of immediacy, collaboration and access to knowledge that their parents did not enjoy in their own youths.

This increasing potential for self-advocacy and access to information, together with a series of high-profile failings of governance in institutions and business across the world, has given birth to another phenomenon impacting on the workplace – that is the 'Death of Deference'.[3] Individuals have lost faith in experts, institutions and authority figures as they have grown used to the greater level of self-determinism afforded to them by the internet. People can become expert in almost any field, organize themselves and find a platform for their viewpoints. This is apparent in the rise of petitioning websites such as 38degrees.co.uk, the way that we Google our symptoms and potential treatments before an appointment with the family doctor, and the huge uprisings involving revolution in 2010 in 17 North African and Middle Eastern countries in the space of six months – the 'Arab Spring'. People, both as citizens and consumers, have grown used to having their say and exercising their discretion outside of the workplace and are looking to replicate these conditions within it.

Against this background of rapid change and complexity, the inherited models of the Industrial Revolution start to creak. Service and production models are changing to accommodate the desire for consumers to get involved. Consumers are orientating to a more personal purchasing experience where they can customize their product and work with small teams of 'real' people who facilitate their choices. The youth clothing industry has been one of the earliest to identify this demand where it is common for consumers to get involved in the design of goods. This makes for a small batch production model that is a world away from huge assembly lines. The advent of the home 3d printer will, no doubt, accelerate this move towards a personalized relationship to consumer goods. And these changes are not limited to manufacturing. Workers in a globalized operation may now find themselves in small teams, working remotely across diverse languages, cultures and operating contexts. Recent work by the UK's Chartered Management Institute predicting changes by 2020 states:

> Reflecting the impact of new technologies like social media, managers expect to see more global working and more product development driven by customer input (83% and 77% respectively).[4]

What these new working conditions have in common is a high level of unpredictability that requires flexibility, resilience and innovation within the worker, together with some rather evolved social skills. The Industrial

Model of tightly engineered work regimes, fine divisions of labour, repetition and specialisms militate against the responsiveness and agility required to face this modern work context. All of this points towards deep change and reinvention of everything that we have come to understand as management – the question is what should the new design look like?

Work in the Head

As manufacturing changes, alongside it has grown the so-called knowledge economy. While we wait for the world to settle upon an agreed definition of what this term precisely means, it is a widely held consensus that the modern operating environment needs to be met with innovation and creativity and that the entities that can utilize their intellectual assets effectively will gain a competitive advantage.

Here are some definitions of the knowledge economy:

> The knowledge society is a larger concept than just an increased commitment to R&D. It covers every aspect of the contemporary economy where knowledge is at the heart of value added – from high tech manufacturing and ICTs through knowledge intensive services to the overtly creative industries such as media and architecture.[5] (Kok Report, 2004)

> The knowledge driven economy is not just a new set of high-tech industries such as software and biotechnology, which have built on a science base. Nor is it just a set of new technologies: information technology and the Internet, for example. The knowledge driven economy is about a set of new sources of competitive advantage, particularly the ability to innovate, create new products and exploit new markets, which apply to all industries, high-tech and low-tech, manufacturing and services, retailing and agriculture. In all industries the key to competitiveness increasingly turns on how people combine, marshal and commercialise their know-how.
> That know-how can come from many sources, from shop-floor improvements to quality and productivity, sales staff ideas to serve customers better, as well as from 'knowledge workers': designers, technologists and scientists.[6] (New measures for the New Economy, report by Charles Leadbeater, June 1999)

> Economic success is increasingly based on the effective utilization of intangible assets such as knowledge, skills and innovative potential as the key resource for competitive advantage. The term 'knowledge economy' is used to describe this emerging economic structure. (Economic and Social Research Council, 2005)

The implications for the workplace arising from the emergence of the Knowledge Economy are paradigm shifting. In our industrial past, factory-owning employers owned, in Marxist terms, the 'means of production', and workers had only their physical labour to trade for a wage. As work was fairly unskilled, so workers were interchangeable and had relatively little individual power. This allowed for employers to dictate workplace culture for two and a half centuries.

In the knowledge economy, where thought, individuality, creativity and expertise are valuable commodities, then it must surely follow that, with regards to the commodity of thought, workers now own the means of production. In this way, the means of production are, to some extent, the experiences, beliefs and processes that belong to the individual that the employer hopes to access in search of competitive advantage. This also means that workers are now individually more valuable and can take their knowledge commodities with them. This might even entail setting up in competition with their employer as manufacturing moves to a smaller scale and technology allows for groups of individuals to organize themselves into collectives with increased purchasing power.

We only need to look at the world of book publishing to see how traditional printing in factory conditions has declined, and authors are electing to self publish electronic books direct to the market. The author no longer has to engage a publisher in order to get access to the marketplace. The governing factor is the ability to generate content, which resides with the author. The power dynamic has, to some extent, reversed and we predict that, as manufacturing costs continue to fall, then the asset value of knowledge will rise correspondingly. We are calling this type of labour, 'Work in the Head'.

Work in the Head and the generation of ideas, among other things, requires:

- stimulation;
- provocation;
- variety and diversity of perspective;
- time;
- discussion;
- collaboration; and
- freedom to explore and test hypotheses.

Importantly, it draws upon the experiences that have contributed to the construction of our selves. It is sporadic and sometimes fickle and not containable within notions of working hours. Work in the Head needs a constant

TABLE 2.1 How the requirements of Work in the Head differ from Work in the Hand

Work in the Hand	Work in the Head
Restricted to specific locations	Always with us, not dependent upon location
Standardized (templates, systems, models)	Constantly changing and adapting to shifting circumstances
Focus on activity and filling every moment with production	Focus on mental effort, invention, possibilities and sense making
Minimization of mental distraction and 'time-wasting'	Personal investment using life experiences as material
Simplicity, reproducibility and efficiency	Embracing complexity and valuing individuality
Means of production owned by employers	Means of production owned by workers

exchange of ideas and the removal of structures of deference that may inhibit the freedom of workers to offer their ideas and opinions to those in more senior roles. In short, Work in the Head requires the opposite conditions that our industrial heritage has created (see Table 2.1 for a recap).

And so employers must now be engaged in a process of attracting valuable workers and fostering the conditions that allow them to apply their knowledge and ideas to their full potential. However, many are still mired in the traditions of the last century. To make matters worse, the same old working conditions are geared to a very different working model. In short, many workplaces have the wrong tools for the wrong job and most workers are caught in this double bind.

Caught in a double bind

For most people in employment, there is an internal war being waged for their attention, between work and private life. It is a war that cannot be won within the context of the prevailing culture, as there is an expectation that both domains require full dedication, while placing competing demands upon the individual. The deal in the workplace is that, in return for a wage, commitment must be given to the employer to execute given tasks to the fullness of the ability of the worker. In the instance of serious failures in this obligation on the part of the worker, penalties can be applied which in turn may impact upon the private life and future plans of the employee. In competition with the demands of the employer are the obligations and duties that spring from private life. As parents, children, siblings, friends and members of the community, the requirement to give our best effort is no less than that of the workplace. The consequences of failing to meet the demands of this sphere can also be serious in extreme cases.

And, of course, there is the obligation that the individual has themselves to live a life with some degree of authenticity. The importance of this last point cannot be understated, as the ability to act in accordance with our beliefs and to make our own sense of the world is what gives meaning to our existence:

> The separation of work life from family life has existed since the Industrial
> Revolution and remains largely intact today, even though it has never reflected
> the way most people live. The business world has responded to work-family
> issues with an array of programs and policies that address specific family needs,
> but it does not change this basic assumption that employees' work and private
> lives are separate and conflicting.[7] (Rapoport and Baylin 1996)

We believe that people in paid work are often faced with an impossible conundrum that may not be resolved unless we cease to view work and private life as entirely separate domains. Work and private life are interwoven within our minds as one informs the other. A parent with a sick child will not be able to give their full attention to their paid work, and in the same way, the prospect of a difficult meeting on a Monday morning will cast a shadow over a relaxing Sunday afternoon with friends and family. Likewise, the strategy for how to manage a potentially difficult meeting can come to us on the sidelines of our daughter's football match just as easily as at our desk.

In fact, the concept that employers can purchase a time-share in the mental processes of the individual between agreed working hours is fundamentally wrong-headed, and the resulting strain that is put upon the worker in trying to hold these two worlds apart can often result in compromised health and well-being. There is another point to be made here about the right of employers to interrupt the processes that contribute to self-fulfilment and the creation of meaning in the life of the individual during work hours. We do not believe that paid work and the active process of giving meaning to one's life are incompatible and we will discuss how to bring them together later in the book.

We examine the challenges of conducting Work in the Head in an environment that, for many years, has been shaped by Work in the Hand. We focus on four key areas:

- the duality of life as an employee;
- emotional labour;
- the cost of stress; and
- the work–life balance experiment.

The duality of life as an employee

A change takes place within most of us when we enter our workplace and begin our paid work, and for many it begins with our choice of clothing even before we have left our homes.

We discard our private selves and don our work personas in the process of conforming to the norms of the workplace. Somewhere along our journey to work, we make changes and adjustments to our language, demeanour, sense of identity, appearance, as a host of assumptions and customs begin to act upon us. The sense of the divide between paid work and our private lives is no more keenly felt than during this process of remaking ourselves in preparation for entering into work.

This is not to assert that our private lives are free from expectations and obligations that act to define us to some extent, but it is safe to say that in most cases, we have a far greater degree of choice and self-determinism. Even those who have managed to create or locate paid work that allows for a great deal of self expression can find that there are times when their dealings with the norms of client or supplier workplace cultures will constrain their own choices about how to conduct themselves.

Most people, for example, will wear formal office attire for a job interview or to meet a corporate client for the first time. The semiotic value of a suit and tie cannot be underestimated, and carries within it the whole philosophy of our industrialized past. It describes ideas of uniformity and standardization, efficiency, minimization of distracting choices and reproducibility.

Table 2.2 highlights the divide we create within ourselves by holding apart these two domains.

TABLE 2.2 How we divide ourselves between the private self and the work persona

Work persona	Private self
Dress to suit workplace culture and brand	Dress to suit mood, taste and identity
Impersonal, standardized language	Speech includes dialect, slang, feelings
Corporate	Individual
Belonging to an organization	Belonging to a diverse range of groups and allegiances
Limited dissent; possibly deferential	Free articulation of views
Part of a system	Self-determining
Suppression of authentic self	Potential for liberation of authentic self

The duality of working life does not only extend to how we look and speak. Inroads are being made by the world of work into the private world of our emotions. The rise of the service industry has created another potential schism within the individual as elements of personality are commoditized in exchange for payment. In addition to the demand for physical labour and cognitive labour is increasingly a requirement for 'emotional labour' from employees.

Emotional labour

Organizational sociologist Arlie Hochschild first developed the concept of 'Emotional Labour'.[8] She described the work performed by any service employee who is required, as part of his or her job, to display specific sets of emotions (both verbal and nonverbal) with the aim of inducing particular feelings and responses among those for whom the service is being provided. In this respect, employees are required to control and use their own emotions in order to influence the emotional state of others. The 'service with a smile' approach is a neat example of this. Emotional labour is distinct from the emotional work that we undertake in our private lives, as it is work for which we are paid.

Hochschild describes that certain workplace activities carry with them 'feeling rules' or acceptable emotional display requirements, such as that of a funeral director to appear compassionate towards their clients. In order to observe the given feeling rules of a situation, individuals must engage in emotional acting. The labour, in this example, is in the effort that is needed to constantly detect, define and construct the required emotional response in order to create the desired effect in the customer. Hochschild identified two types of acting in the workplace:

- 'Deep acting' which refers to the process of matching real experienced feeling to the prevailing 'feeling rule'. In this way the funeral director may be moved by the real grief displayed by their client to feel authentic compassion. Alternatively, the funeral director might need to employ a form of method acting whereby they access a memory of past emotional experiences to produce the required feeling. In this instance the funeral director may remember how they felt when they themselves lost a close relative, allowing them to access their compassion in compliance with the feeling rule.

- 'Surface acting' refers to the expression of an emotion that is not, at any level, genuinely felt. In this example, the funeral director may show the surface signs of compassion but perhaps because they have recently received distracting news or because they judge the client to be rude, their apparent compassion would be in the absence of an authentic emotion.

The following consequences can arise from engaging in emotional labour, such as:

- it can be an exhausting and depleting process for the worker, who is required to mine their hitherto private emotional domain for 'goods' to sell in the workplace, which can lead to harmful emotional states;

- emotional dissonance, that is a feeling of being disconnected from one's emotions, can arise from a prolonged period of surface acting emotional labour;

- depersonalization may follow as a defensive measure against emotional dissonance whereby, in order to cope with the strain of emotional exhaustion, the individual will decrease their personal investment in their emotions and those of others. This can ultimately act as a barrier to deep acting authentic emotion resulting in a vicious cycle; and

- in extreme cases the individual may experience emotional burnout and their ability to regulate their emotions becomes highly impaired.

Blake Ashforth and Ronald Humphrey described a distinction between the impact of deep acting emotional labour, which allows for authentic emotional expression, and surface acting emotional labour that can alienate the individual from their genuine emotional responses:

> If emotional labour is consistent with a central, salient, and valued social and/or personal identity (or identities), it will lead to enhanced psychological wellbeing [...] If emotional labour is inconsistent [...], it will lead to emotive dissonance and/or a loss of one's sense of authentic self.[9]

The job of emotional labour though is not the preserve of client-facing workers, as managers and leaders alike (and many other sections of the workforce too) are routinely engaged in this form of labour as they set out motivating, connecting to, inspiring and confronting colleagues in the work they do. And the 'shadow' that senior people cast on the organization places an extra responsibility associated with being watched and scrutinized for the actions they take. In all of this, the same risks of emotional exhaustion, burnout, dissonance and defensiveness are entertained by scores of workers every day.

The cost of stress

The duality of working life sets up particular strains within the worker. The ongoing process of suppressing elements of our identity and vetting thought, behaviour and emotion, while conforming to unhelpful workplace norms erodes our authenticity and fragments us.

As illustrated, one of the consequences of workplace duality is stress, and it sits alongside other stress triggers such as excessive working hours, toxic managers and so on. According to the UK Health and Safety Executive's Stress and Psychological Disorders in Great Britain 2013, the Labour Force Survey for 2011 to 2012 revealed that 10.4 million working days were lost to stress-related illness in the UK. The average number of days off work for each person suffering with this condition in this period was 24, one of the highest days lost per case figures for any of the recognized health complaints in the survey.

This is in no way peculiar to the UK. The American Institute of Stress states that numerous studies find job stress to be the major source of stress for American adults and that it has increased progressively over the past few decades. This has serious consequences for health and well-being:

> Increased levels of job stress as assessed by the perception of having little control but lots of demands have been demonstrated to be associated with increased rates of heart attack, hypertension and other disorders.[10]

It goes on to describe that when police officers from New York, Los Angeles and other municipalities suffer a coronary event in the line of duty, or even when on vacation, it is automatically considered to be a work-related injury and compensated accordingly. Such is the level of acceptance of the relationship between job stress and heart attacks.

The World Health Organization states: 'Work-related stress is an issue of growing concern in developing countries due to processes of globalization and the changing nature of work.'[11]

The impact of work-related stress is not only endured by the individual. There is a great deal written about the cost to business and economies, but the people and relationships that revolve around the individual are also affected in ways that can sometimes be hidden from the rest of us. The outside world may not able to see or measure the malign influence of workplace stress upon life partners or children. Stressed workers may not contribute to their community because their mental energy is being spent in worry and anxiety.

The work–life balance experiment

Such a serious threat to modern life and economic productivity hasn't gone without equally serious attempts to find a solution. The search for 'work–life balance' has been an earnest and well-intentioned attempt to heal the schism within the working individual. Organizations have made great advances in acknowledging that employees have lives outside of work that are as important to them as their paid employment (often more so). Driven initially by working parents 'juggling' their time between work and family commitments, the opportunities afforded by technological advances have meant that many of us can work from home, or anywhere else that we can find a Wi-Fi signal.

Millennials, the 'digital natives', along with many others, have taken up this desire to blur the geographical lines between work and private life and have added their own brand of technological savvy with social media etc.

This has resulted in a proliferation of points of access to workers but also a sense of 24/7 availability that has been well documented. Increasing globalization has exacerbated this phenomenon as dealing with clients and colleagues from different time zones necessitates the existence of permanent access.

In effect, the solutions to creating greater flexibility have allowed employers to encroach upon private life, which in turn has been eroded in equal measure.

Much of the tension that this generates is due to the fact that the workplace is evolving at a faster pace than workplace norms (that in themselves have been formed over centuries). The result is a tendency to oscillate between our work and private personas at ever increasing rates. For example, we might picture the comic scenario of the executive sat, late at night, at their kitchen table, conducting a Skype call with clients, while they are dressed from the waist up in business attire and from the waist down in nightwear. The urge to create the conditions and expectations of the office, even while sitting at home and ready to go to bed, is so powerful that the resulting behaviour becomes farcical. Even if we don't have overseas clients, there are more of us who surreptitiously check e-mails on holiday than would admit to it, and who would choose to ignore an urgent call from their boss when they are lying under an umbrella on the beach?

Many of those surveyed as part of this book, identified out-of-hours work as a permanent feature of their lives:

I [work] a lot [out of hours]. More than I should, as it isn't always constructive. Sometimes I'm working or planning, but if I'm tired I just worry! (PR Executive)

I find that my thinking about work outside of hours usually occurs when I should be sleeping. I have to manage this so that it doesn't affect my health. It is usually a mix of planning and worrying about my interactions with colleagues. (Executive Education Support)

[I] regularly work out of hours, that is every day, except maybe Saturday ... I am on call and have to respond to email 24/7, even on holidays. I would do some extra work or reading most nights after work, and on Sunday evenings. I have spent many nights in recent months worrying about the difficult restructuring/cost cutting our department is going through. Not very happy at work and it is showing in my demeanour outside of work. (Adviser in large organisation)

I find I have to do quite a lot of research outside of my normal office hours. This often includes learning new software or planning the week ahead for workshops. Because I also live locally to my job I often encounter staff/students

in social settings and they might want to discuss an idea there and then.
(University Technical Adviser)

In another moving account we heard how workplace norms around suppressing certain emotional responses can be damaging to people, and applying the norms of personal life might have a more positive result:

> Years ago, as a reviewer for political asylum applications, I had to interview a woman who had claimed that her husband had been murdered. It was a formal interview with strict procedures and I had to conduct myself to a particular professional standard. She told me that her husband had been murdered by a gang after being dragged from his house. I asked if she had any proof of this to back up her account, expecting her to produce a death certificate or police report or something else like a press cutting. Instead she gave me a Polaroid photograph of severed human heads stacked in a pyramid and pointing to one, said, 'that's my husband'. I was very shocked and upset by this, as I hadn't been expecting it, and felt that I just had to continue with the interview. Afterwards I wanted to speak to my colleagues and take a moment to process what had just happened, but there was a culture of not admitting weakness and 'laughing it off' that meant that I had to keep it to myself. This happened a long time ago, but I find that it still upsets me as I write about it now. (Government worker)

Authenticity is both the problem and the solution

Against this backdrop, the modern work environment leaves us in a state of tension in a number of important respects:

- there is a tension between the old methods of organization born out of the Work in the Hand era (that has dominated our thinking for centuries) and the new methods of organization. These two eras are characterized by 'Work in the Hand' which introduced separate places of work to which we had to travel, standardization of working processes, minimization of variations, the minimization of distraction, and the absorption of all available energy in executing the task etc. 'Work in the Head' in contrast enabled work to happen anywhere, requires personal inventiveness and innovation, emphasizes exploration, the space to think and dialogue, and variation in processes etc.

- There is a tension between the growth in a desire for self-determinism and the strictures and depersonalizing conventions of the workplace. This appetite for self-determinism is catalyzed, among other things, by the educational power of the internet, underlined by the 'death of deference' phenomenon.

- There is a tension between the assumption that work can be held separate from our private life when it increasingly draws on the personal experiences, emotions, passions, individual creativity and intellectual property that characterizes our private life.

- There is a tension between the increasing encroachment of work on the private time of individuals, and the stress that this generates in the individual.

- There is a tension between the equally stringent responsibilities of 'work' and 'home' life and the expectation that they will both be discharged to the individual's best ability.

- There is a tension between the requirement to undertake emotional acting in work and the suppression of genuinely felt emotion in the individual in support of this labour.

As discussed, our proposition in relation to all of this is that it is simply untenable to continue with the idea that we should hold work and home life apart. As long as we do this, and as long we attempt to tolerate conflicting dress codes, languages, forms of expression, norms, values, emotional and intellectual processes, the more we will feel the stress and strain on our authenticity. It is not too dramatic to consider this situation as one of a 'divided self', which the psychiatrist R D Laing outlines:

> If the individual delegates all transactions between himself and the other to a system within his being which is not 'him', then the world is experienced as unreal, and all that belongs to this system is felt to be false, futile, and meaningless.[12]

This alienation from the self is felt particularly keenly when we remind ourselves that most people spend most of their waking hours in work. And for some four billion people working across the world, this issue is worth taking seriously. In this context, this attempt to hold the two worlds apart not only comes at a cost for us personally, but also for organizations in terms of the costs of stress and sick absence, depleted well-being, and low levels of authentic engagement with the organization and its ambitions.

In the remainder of this book we examine strategies for bringing these two worlds closer together and in doing so realizing the significant benefits for the individual and the organization.

Notes

1 de Botton, A (2010) *The Pleasures and Sorrows of Work*, Penguin Books, London, p 35.

2 Trueman, C., The Industrial Revolution, www.historylearningsite.co.uk [online] www.historylearningsite.co.uk/factories_industrial_revolution.htm [accessed 2 February 2014].

3 Ryde, R (2012) *Never Mind the Bosses: Hastening the death of deference for business success*, Wiley & Sons, London.

4 www.managers.org.uk/news/changing-world-work-must-drive-management-makeover

5 Facing the Challenge – The Lisbon Strategy for Growth and Employment, Report for the High Level Group chaired by Wim Kok, Luxembourg November 2004, p 19, http://europa.eu.int/comm/lisbon_strategy/index_en.html

6 New Measures for the New Economy, Report sponsored by the Centre for Business Performance of the Institute of Chartered Accountants in England and Wales, p 7, London, June 1999, www1.oecd.org/sti/ind/1947910.pdf

7 Rapoport, R and Baylin, L (1996) *Relinking Life and Work: Toward a better future*, Pegasus, p 10.

8 Hochschild, AR (1979) *The Managed Heart: Commercialization of human feeling*, University of California Press.

9 Ashforth, B and Humphrey, R (1993) Emotional Labor in Service Roles: The influence of identity, *The Academy of Management Review*, 18, pp 88–115

10 Workplace Stress, The American Institute of Stress, [online] www.stress.org/workplace-stress/ [accessed 19 January 2014].

11 Protecting Workers' Health Series No. 6, Raising awareness of stress at work in developing countries, Irene Houtman and Karin Jettinghoff, TNO Work & Employment, The Netherlands, and Leonor Cedillo, Occupational Health researcher, Mexico © World Health Organization 2007.

12 Laing, RD (1969) *The Divided Self*, Penguin Books, London, p 80.

A design for workplace authenticity

03

Against the backdrop of a work–life that threatens to divide the personality into two warring factions, we turn our attention to how we might design authenticity into the experience of work while driving out the psychological dissonance examined in the previous chapter.

Our starting point on this is clear in that most people spend most of their waking hours in work. And furthermore, most of our adult years see us engaged in paid and non-paid labour.

Work matters a great deal, and we see it as a priority that people are able to be themselves at work, that they should be free to express themselves at work and that they should be free from the dissonance and alienation that work so often creates. The prize that is offered to the individual employee is significant in its own right, and if that were where the story ended, then this would be a truly meaningful and highly worthwhile result. But we also believe that if this is done right then the organizations that we work for stand to benefit in terms of greater engagement, innovation, and productivity. Better still, where there is greater authenticity we believe that organizations will adapt more quickly and much more effectively to the volatile circumstances of the operating environment. This is a 'win-win' that is worth fighting for. The question that remains is what should a design for workplace authenticity look like?

This chapter introduces a model that can be used in all workplaces as both a diagnostic tool and a strategy for creating authenticity. The model is called the 'Freedoms Model' (Figure 3.1), and it is our view that both managers and workers should see it as a priority to bring it to life. The gains are considerable and the principles are simple to follow. As you read this chapter think, at each stage in the process, how your situation and your organization matches up to the ideas presented.

During the following chapters each of these three components of the model will be explained and examined in detail, but in terms of the top-level notions conveyed by each, we define these terms as recapped in Table 3.1.

FIGURE 3.1   The Freedoms Model

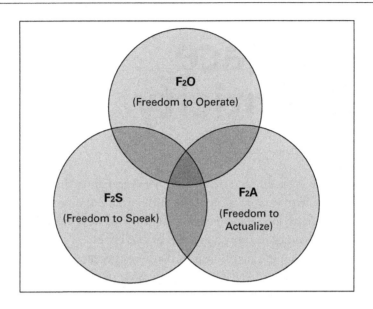

TABLE 3.1   Definition of terms

The Freedom to Operate	The freedom to arrange your affairs in the way you think best to accomplish your goals.
The Freedom to Speak	The freedom to offer your views in a way which isn't censored or constrained by others, in particular by those at higher levels in the hierarchy.
The Freedom to Actualize	The freedom to assume and realize an identity and perspective that is different from others' and reflects your own emergent personality and values.

But this offer is not made lightly. It is recognized that many, if not most, organizations operate through a system of tight management of people and processes so that particular results are achieved. As such, there will understandably be a degree of in-built resistance to the messages and methods offered here that involve both a loosening up of what is in place and a degree of experimentation in the process. It does not, however, stop here. The freedoms being made available are not always going to be embraced by employees in quite the way that might be imagined. Erich Fromm has spoken about this in his work *Escape from Freedom*:

> Is there not also, perhaps, besides an innate desire for freedom, an instinctive wish for submission? If there is not, how can we account for the attraction which submission to a leader has for so many today? Is there [in fact] hidden satisfaction in submitting?[1]

And so we ask that the reader simultaneously appreciate the work that may be involved in this endeavour but also the enormous moral and operational value to be won as a result.

Important guiding forces

For the model to be applied in the way envisaged there are two further variables that need to be brought into play, specifically:

1 The obligations that fall on the individual that accompany each of these freedoms. These might be thought of as the 'contra-entry' to each of these freedoms.

2 The management task that accompanies the model. This represents a new conceptualization of the role of management and is explained in greater depth in Chapter 4.

The obligations that belong to workers accepting these freedoms are important. These will vary but include those set out in Figure 4.1 on page 53.

These obligations come into focus in different ways according to the freedoms that are being exercised. We might think of each of these obligations representing sliders on a mixing desk with the volume being increased or decreased as appropriate.

For example, the more that workers act on the Freedom to Operate (F2O), the more we would expect to see employees appraising themselves of the corporate initiatives under way. Similarly, the more that workers utilize the Freedom to Speak (F2S) and perhaps in doing so engage in discussions about the 'elephant in the room', the more they need to deploy skill, sensitivity and be aware of the consequences for others in doing so. Finally, as workers take steps to enact their Freedom to Actualize (F2A) the more thought that might need to go into the impact on, and implications for, the ethics and values of the organization.

TABLE 3.2 Six key obligations for the individual that accompany the Freedoms Model

1	Corporate awareness	The obligation to engage with the corporate messages and priorities of the organization so that freedoms are taken in full awareness of these, eg attendance and participation in formal corporate communication sessions such as 'town hall' meetings
2	Ethics and values	The obligation to honour the ethics and values of the organization when acting on freedoms
3	Learning	The obligation to proactively share the success or otherwise of acting on the freedoms
4	Risk	The obligation to undertake 'de-risking' activity when attempting new and novel approaches, eg committing to making small changes and learning quickly rather than making big changes without first establishing the value of the change
5	Consequential awareness	The obligation to build understanding (and act on this) of the potential impact of changes and actions arising from freedoms, eg the knock-on effect to other people and roles
6	Accountability	The obligation to accept accountability for actions that arise from accepting freedoms

In transactional analysis terms, our position on the obligations resting with workers, is to treat employees as 'adults' and not, as often found in organizations, for managers to assume the role of 'parents', and in doing so to cast workers in the role of 'children'. A rule of thumb that captures the obligations that first belong to managers, and second belong to workers is 'Stand back (managers), and step up (workers)' but importantly both need to be present.

The management task that is allied to the Freedoms Model is explored later and so details are provided there. However, as an indication of what might be involved, there are five areas in which managers should be particularly active which relate to all three freedoms:

- assisting in modelling AUTHENTICITY and removing barriers for others;

- assisting in facilitating learning and ADAPTATION as new ways of being, and doing business are found;

- assisting in achieving ALIGNMENT between broader corporate imperatives and the freedoms that are enacted locally;

- assisting in securing ACCOUNTABILITY in the local enactment of freedoms; and

- on occasion intervening and taking ACTION where conduct or ideas do not support the three freedoms.

The philosophical position that we take

The management task, and the responsibility that sits with the organization as a whole to support authenticity, is important. Let's be clear that full success depends on leaders, managers and workers alike playing their role.

But our position on authenticity is that responsibility for claiming it must ultimately rest with the individual. Our philosophical perspective, to the extent that we offer one, has shades of Libertarianism. We see people as self-governing individuals who make choices and are responsible for them. Authenticity is rightly a concern for all, but it is for the individual to define it for themselves, to strive to attain it (should they choose to), and importantly to resist giving way to the temptation that it is the job of management to furnish it for them. My authenticity sits with me, yours with you, and it is not our belief that it is anyone's responsibility to find it or 'fix it' for someone else.

It is for this reason that we frame the central 'solution' to the puzzle of authenticity as a series of freedoms – the Freedom to Operate, the Freedom to Speak and the Freedom to Actualize. These are freedoms that, as with all freedoms, need to be constructed, navigated and claimed as much as they might be given.

It is Karpman's 'Drama Triangle' that provides a useful means of illustrating some of the dangers of adopting a less self-empowered position. We borrow this concept to shed a little light on our approach towards finding authenticity. The Drama Triangle, which is drawn from the field of transactional analysis, describes an observed psychological game involving three roles – the victim, the persecutor and the rescuer. The situation plays out when a person takes a role as victim or persecutor. Others then take up the remaining roles. All three roles are self-serving and the rescuer, for example, is more interested in adopting a position that satisfies their ego and in being seen as 'the person that rescues the victim' than they are in resolving the tension. Similarly the victim takes their position in justifying certain emotional needs such as needing to feel angry or 'hard done by'. The persecutor gets to feel safe by hurting and exerting power over others. The melodrama is dynamic and positions are frequently switched with the rescuer, for example, swapping with the persecutor and so on. Claude Steiner illustrates the falsehood that belies each role: 'The victim is not really as helpless as he feels, the rescuer is not really helping, and the persecutor does not really have a valid complaint.'[2]

When it comes to authenticity our aim is to break out of a cycle we see being repeated in organizations (to jump off the Drama Triangle). The cycle is one where workers and managers respectively find themselves assuming the roles of victim and persecutor, and they remain locked in a battle of pushing responsibility back and forth between each other. Both parties feel justified in handing responsibility to the other and so the game goes on. But to focus on the victim, Claude Steiner captures the possibility here in the words 'the victim is not really as helpless as he feels'. As the owner of their authenticity, it is the individual who must take primary responsibility. And of course the manager, who we might think of as being cast in the position of persecutor (which refers also to behaviours of providing pressure and coercion), is an individual too, and their authenticity belongs to them. So in practice we would expect to see both sides of the equation working furiously to make this a success because of the significant benefits arising from greater authenticity that flow to the individual(s) and to the organization.

A final element to the philosophy that accompanies this book is our appreciation of the Existentialist argument. The Existential point of view, as articulated by people such as Camus and Sartre, is captured in part by the proposition that 'existence precedes essence'. What this means is that there are no pre-existing determinants of what we are as humans and what we should be. Our moral code, for example, is ours to construct. It is not something that we should take from others. The way we conduct our interactions with people or our encounters with the world are based on the choices that we make to do this. The Existentialist perspective favours the notion of a *Tabula Rasa* (meaning 'blank slate' in Latin) when considering human understanding. We do not arrive pre-shaped, pre-destined or pre-scripted;

our thinking about the purpose of our lives and how we should live our lives is fully governed by our own choices and decisions. And furthermore, the Existentialist argument moves beyond the point of our choices and our thinking, and concludes that action, which is consistent with our thinking, *must* then arise. If I believe it is wrong to eat meat, then I must not eat meat. If I believe that a war in the Gulf is wrong I must take action. If I believe that I should be more authentic at work, then I must act on this.

The following chapters focus on the *freedoms* that we have to be authentic, and this particular focus is deliberate. Some people may have a wide scope and freedom to be authentic while others will have less. The importance of centring the discussion on the freedom to be authentic rather than authenticity itself is to remain true to the philosophy set out here. Authenticity will be 'filled up' by action, and freedoms will be exercised or not. In each chapter we encourage creative challenge of the boundaries of these freedoms, and we also challenge managers to play their role in facilitating authenticity, but the space that freedom offers needs to be stepped into by each and every one of us. Our hope is that this opportunity is grabbed with both hands and this leads to organizations and workplaces that exude authenticity from every pore, and in every movement made.

Notes

1 Fromm, E (1965) *Escape from Freedom*, Holt Paperbacks, p 5.
2 Steiner, C (1979) *Healing Alcoholism*, Grove Press, p 208.

The first freedom
The Freedom to Operate

" *Prior to my current job I would have said that work was something of a hindrance and a constraint but I now see it as something that enhances my life and [gives me] a sense of purpose... It came about through the realisation that I had the opportunity to start with a blank slate and write my own job description, which was a bit daunting initially. Once I realised how much faith and trust had been placed in me by management, I felt empowered to go on and make it a job that would be something enjoyable and get the best out of me.*

UNIVERSITY STUDENT SUPPORT/ADVISER

It is understandable that organizations should want to invest so much of their time and money, as they do, in selecting the right candidates for the positions available within the organization. The same would apply, for example, to the often-lengthy processes and governance procedures surrounding promotion and reward. Getting these right matters not least because organizations live with the consequences and often for many years.

The people that walk through the doors of the enterprise therefore do so for the first time having been specified, selected, assessed, measured, longlisted, shortlisted and eventually judged right for the organization. And having arrived in the organization the same people are typically trained and developed and equipped to do the job, and not just once but continually throughout their careers. And to keep them on course, they are loaded up on a weekly diet of corporate information, they are managed by those more senior to them, and they are provided with the tools, the team members and the assets to do the job they are paid to do.

And yet despite this, very many employees find themselves not feeling that they have the room that they need to operate. The trust that you hope would arise from these quality assurance processes somehow gets lost in translation. The job of management, which in many ways embodies an implicit lack of confidence in employees, involves ensuring compliance not only to the standards and results expected, but also in large part to the stated ways in which workers conduct their business. Warren Bennis, who offers a definition of the difference between leadership and management, illustrates this compliance point well: 'leaders do the right things, while managers do things right'. In short, it would seem that almost every effort is made by our organizations to stop employees doing the very thing they have been recruited to do and this is a major flaw in how we frame the roles of both employees and managers.

Across Europe workers express concern about the limited degree of control that they have about important decisions relating to their work. The European Working Conditions Survey provides one illustration of this point with a low proportion of respondents (between 28 and 58 per cent) reporting that they were able to affect decisions important for their work/ organization of their work.

Focusing in on Britain, a recent report (2012) by the UK's Economic and Social Research Council and the UK Commission for Employment and Skills concluded that:

> The proportion of employees who report that they have a great deal or quite
> a lot of say over work organisation declined from 36% to 27% between 2001
> and 2012...[and] employees' ability to influence decisions at work is one of the
> most important factors affecting their motivation and psychological well-being.[1]

The notion of a causal relationship between job control and psychological well-being has been studied on various occasions. A particular formulation of this relationship was developed by Karasek in 1979 and described as the 'Job Demand-Control model'. Karasek proposed that well-being could be negatively affected by low job control and that this was exacerbated by the level of demand that the job introduces. For example, where low decision latitude is matched by high job demand, the effects can be negative in the extreme, giving rise to significant psychological strain. Karasek named this the 'strain hypothesis' and this concept has been used to explain, among other things, the terrible circumstances and psychological processes related to 'Shellshock' during the First World War.

The 2010 European Working Conditions Survey found that, when measuring employee perceptions of their involvement in decision-making relating to their work, the majority of respondents from 26 of the 35 countries surveyed felt unable to influence or were not involved in these kinds of decisions. Of those countries that reported a more positive state of affairs, the survey still found over 40 per cent of respondents reported feeling a lack of involvement or influence in the decision-making process.

Our proposition though is that not only should we seek to minimize the negative consequences for workers (in the form of psychological strain) from a narrow Freedom to Operate, but that the opposite can be achieved (in the form of high motivation, greater ownership and so on) by introducing a broad Freedom to Operate. This, we will go on to argue, is true across all types of jobs even where they ostensibly appear to be lower in demand/complexity and with jobs that would seem to offer up limited opportunities to expand the Freedom to Operate.

Definition and dimensions

The Freedom to Operate (F2O) identified in the Freedoms Model involves allowing employees to reach their own judgements on the best strategies for fulfilling the tasks they face, and being allowed to execute on this basis.

The question of how the work should be tackled is one that rests firmly with the employee. But more than this, even when it comes to alternative conceptualizations about what the task itself should entail, this too should be in the domain of control of the individual. The key idea is that employees are both invited and trusted to be creative in the way they shape and deliver their work. Under this model, the freedoms that they might claim in relation to this could be manifest in a range of ways. For example, some workers may make particular judgements about the timing and pacing of activities in their portfolio. Others may want to form particular partnerships or collaborations in order to accomplish their work. Judgements might be made about the best style or modus operandi to employ to achieve the results required. Some workers may choose to deploy technology in support of their aims or alternatively select face-to-face communications as their primary strategy. All of these choices are available to, and in the gift of, the workers to whom the tasks belong.

Other ways in which people can exercise their Freedom to Operate include:

- the outputs delivered to meet the organization's mission;
- the processes used to deliver outputs/outcomes;

- the relationships that are built and utilized to deliver results;
- the extent to which tasks are delivered using internal vs external capabilities/capacity;
- the degree of involvement and collaboration with other divisions in the business; and
- the extent to which customers are recruited in the process of production, eg the way that Ikea customers build their own furniture and supermarket shoppers bag their own purchases.

Implicit in all of this is an ongoing process of research, experimentation and engagement in service of finding the best solutions. Importantly though, this is driven and 'owned' by the employee rather than being directed or prescribed by the manager. It is empowering in the truest sense of the word and accompanying this level of freedom is the authenticity and 'alignment with self' for which we are searching.

Importantly though, these freedoms need to be matched by the obligations outlined in Figure 4.1. This should not be thought of as a 'free for all' or an invitation to create chaos. Such is the fear that typically exists in relation to this risk, that most organizations would rather disempower and disengage their employees than build their capability in accepting responsibility and taking the initiative. The Freedoms Model alongside the individual obligations and management task is the remedy to this sad state of affairs.

Benefits of the Freedom to Operate

The benefits of enabling employees to have the Freedom to Operate are considerable. We might think of these as falling into two categories reflecting whether the benefits accrue to the individual or to the organization.

At the individual level, greater Freedom to Operate can give rise to:

- a sense of feeling trusted (which arises from being afforded the freedom to make important decisions with support being offered from above to help make this happen);
- greater pride in the work done (as employees are allowed to craft their own solutions, they are able to take greater pride in the results that they have created);
- high levels of motivation (which are directly related to the opportunity to meaningfully apply one's own thoughts and experience to the task in hand);

- the ability to leverage one's own particular strengths to the job (accompanying the Freedom to Operate is also the ability to select and deploy individual strengths to the task. In other situations where there is less Freedom to Operate workers may feel that they have to work 'against type');

- engagement (the more people are personally invested in their work, the greater the level of engagement that is likely to be generated);

- self-expression and greater authenticity (the more control that is experienced in the execution of work, the more people are able to express themselves and be themselves in their work); and

- much greater learning (discussed below).

At the level of the organization, greater Freedom to Operate can give rise to:

- Greater resourcefulness and innovation (as workers seek to source solutions to their own issues and feel able to freely explore a greater range of possibilities, their resourcefulness, creativity and innovation increases. Not only does this deliver a benefit to the task but it also raises capability across, and for, the organization).

- Employees having more 'skin in the game' and therefore more commitment to the success of the organization (too often employees find themselves in the 'consent and evade' space where, for example, they ostensibly accept corporate messages and initiatives but in practice do not truly feel responsible for them. The freedoms approach inspires workers to commit in ways that breeds engagement and greater interest in the organization's success).

- Greater accountability and ownership in the workplace (as employees find ways to express themselves in their work, and engage more fully in their work, they also build a greater sense of ownership about what they and others do in the workplace. And as workers feel more responsible for the results they create, so do they feel more accountable for the product of their efforts).

- Agility and adaptability in the face of changing circumstances (employees that are highly motivated are continually looking for options to improve their work, and because they are located close to the 'coal face' they are able to detect and respond to changes in the environment, such as shifts in customer expectations. They are also better equipped to see and act upon opportunities).

- High productivity (we know from the work of Daniel Pink and David McClelland that autonomy and the opportunity to make an impact is a key driver of productivity.[2] The Freedom to Operate provides the ideal circumstances to support both of these aspirations).

- Much greater learning (discussed below).

In relation to these benefits there are two areas that warrant particular attention, namely trust and the learning benefits.

Trust is a much-discussed topic in organizational life and for good reason. It is important to employees that they feel trusted to act. The Freedom to Operate clearly speaks to the heart of this and in order for freedoms to be allowed senior managers must trust their employees. But trust also flows from junior to more senior levels and this acts, or can act, as a virtuous cycle. However trust in senior managers is very often not felt:

> Trust is an economic issue. If employees do not trust their leaders, this damages business performance. Employees spend more time covering their backs and trying to second-guess what management are up to. They are much less likely to be engaged in their work; indeed, they are more likely to be looking for another job and are unlikely to recommend their employer to anyone else... But little over a third of the UK workforce say they trust their leaders and another third at least need convincing, which means they are likely to question the motivation for change and wonder if there is a hidden agenda. Employers can't afford a lack of trust to hold them back.[3] (Mark Beatson, Chief Economist, Chartered Institute of Personnel Development (CIPD))

We see the application of the Freedom to Operate as a critical step that can start to break the cycle of mistrust between managers and workers (in both directions). And in doing so there lies the opportunity to reap the lost benefits highlighted above.

Furthermore, we see other downsides to a mode of management and leadership that demands compliance (and that operates on a basis of limited Freedom to Operate).

During crises (which may be one of the few instances in which command is appropriate) doing what you are told to do may be the smartest and most appropriate strategy. When an accident occurs on the motorway and emergency vehicles need to quickly gain access to the site, it is appropriate that drivers are directed, without prevarication, to clear the path and to get out of the way. And at the time, and certainly in this example, this is right. But this, along with other organizationally relevant examples of being given firm instruction, does not generate much in the way of learning. Responding in the moment and doing exactly as required delivers the opposite of learning in that little or no mental effort is required to comply. In the same way, where there are very limited options or perhaps just one option for you to adopt, you are less likely to innovate, to invent or even to feel ownership over the option you enact.

However, when you are offered the Freedom to Operate in your work environment this requires that you bring everything that you can to solve the problems to hand. Very much like the practice of coaching, the coach does not provide the answers to the issues that the coachee presents, rather they pose questions that inspire deep reflection and the create the freedom to respond. Look at these three examples of questions (relating to work–life balance) and consider which provides greater freedom to respond, and which is likely to generate the best learning:

Option A: Have you considered working less?

Option B: Which is more important to you, your home or work-life?

Option C: What would need to happen for you to have a better work–
life balance?

In this example, Option C generates a higher level of enquiry and learning, and is the equivalent to introducing greater Freedom to Operate (albeit here within the frame of a conversation).

This notion of personally motivated enquiry supported by the Freedom to Operate is recognized in many quarters to be one of the best ways to learn and grow. Carl Rogers, the influential American psychologist, gives his view on this:

> I have come to believe that the only learning which significantly influences
> behaviour is self-discovered, self-appropriated learning.[4] (Carl Rogers, 1989)

This, however, starts to highlight the benefit to the individual in terms of learning and growth, but the benefit is felt just as powerfully at the organizational level.

In the modern operating environment changes occur quickly and, it would seem, increasingly so. The American 'organizational psychologist' Kurt Lewin, developed in 1947 a change model known as the three-stage change process. The first stage involved 'unfreezing' the organization from its existing habits, mindset and strategies. Stage two was about determining the desired form and shape for the organization, and then the third stage was about re-freezing the organization in its new form and sending it off into the world. This model, like much of Lewin's thinking, has great depth beyond this top-level description, but nevertheless, this is the essence of the idea. While this model continues to provide great service to organizations looking to change, I would like to suggest a different notion that reflects the modern condition and that is of 'slushy change'. In the modern world because of the pace of change, the degree of interdependence between variables and the level of unpredictability, the organization rarely manages to re-freeze in its new state before another major cause for change comes along. Organizations find themselves in a permanently slushy state of being where the ice never fully re-freezes.

In this context, learning and the ability to learn (at the individual and the organizational level) takes on a new level of importance. In fact, one could characterize attitudes to change as having gone through three stages that, over time, have afforded greater emphasis to learning:

- Stage 1: Better mastery over change, eg as we might find demonstrated by the work of Kotter.
- Stage 2: Better at complex change in an environment of rapid change, eg valuing the ability to fail fast, learn, adapt and move on.
- Stage 3: Building 'Adaptive Capability' – with a clear focus on shaping organizations (including systems, people, cultures, processes etc) so that they are agile, ready and able to face unimagined change.

The Freedoms to Operate element of the broader Freedoms Model is designed to support Stages 2 and 3 and to build in learning to organizational life.

The Absolute Freedom to Operate and Residual Freedom to Operate

It is clear that organizations differ in their appetite for autonomy. For example, the degree of Freedom to Operate that we would expect from a nuclear power plant would be different from that of an advertising agency. Similarly, the Freedom to Operate that we would expect to see enjoyed by a judge in a court of law would be different from that of an investigating police detective where greater creativity and exploration might be required.

In this sense, it is useful to think of the Freedom to Operate as comprising two important elements, namely:

- The Absolute Freedom to Operate (AF2O); and
- The Residual Freedom to Operate (RF2O).

FIGURE 4.1 An illustration of different Absolute and Residual Freedoms to Operate according to organizational type and individual role

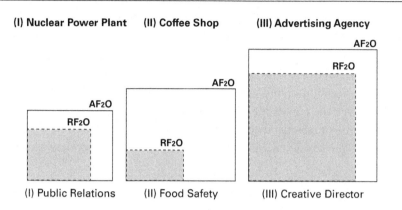

The Absolute Freedom to Operate refers to the outer limit of possibility/acceptability (of the Freedom to Operate) that is associated with the organizational context. High safety environments, for example, would typically have a narrow Absolute Freedom to Operate.

The Residual Freedom to Operate refers to the outer limit of possibility/acceptability (of the Freedom to Operate) that is associated with the role being examined. Highly creative roles, for example, may have a broad Residual Freedom to Operate.

Figure 4.1 offers some scenarios in which we might witness the starting point of an analysis of the Absolute Freedom to Operate and the Residual Freedom to Operate.

As the diagram illustrates, in the case of a Nuclear Power Plant (I) we might conceive of there being a relatively narrow Absolute Freedom to Operate. By this we mean that there will understandably be many fixed features to how business has to be conducted that reflect the discipline of working in a high safety/high risk environment, and one that attracts heavy regulatory attention. By comparison we might think of a coffee shop (II) as enjoying a comparatively greater degree of Absolute Freedom to Operate. That said, this will be mediated by the physical limitations of the shop itself, the narrow range of products/services being offered, and perhaps if it is a chain coffee store, then there will be standardized elements to the appearance, service, quality and so on. With regard to an Advertising Agency (III) we can imagine that there would be a much greater Absolute Degree of Freedom to Operate compared to the other two organization types.

Focusing though on the roles that employees undertake, we may encounter a very different, and arguably more important, profile that we call the Residual Freedom to Operate. Taking the example of a Nuclear Power Plant (I), while in general we can reasonably surmise that Freedoms to Operate may be limited, within this frame there will be roles, such as that of Public Relations, where the Freedom to Operate may be significant. We might also see that by comparison to that of a Food Safety Officer in a Coffee Shop (II), the Public Relations Officer in the Nuclear Power Plant will have a broader range of possibilities and variables of play with, and so on.

However, the reason for describing this as the 'starting point of an analysis' is that in both instances of the Absolute and the Residual Freedom to Operate, our strong encouragement in applying the Freedoms Model is as follows:

- As far as possible, you should creatively challenge any limiting assumptions about the Absolute Freedom to Operate. An example of this would be in relation to the work of the Fire and Rescue services where, in many jurisdictions, they have broadened their Absolute Freedom to Operate through challenging their role as a service that puts out fires to one that prevents fires from occurring in the first instance. In doing this, Fire and Rescue Services increase their Freedom to Operate and the public value that they deliver. In this example this has led to a significant decrease in fire callouts and fire deaths. The key to doing this well is to start with a clear sense of the organization's mission and to consider the various ways in which this can be satisfied and the possibilities this creates (see Figure 4.2).

- As far as possible, you should creatively challenge any limiting assumptions about the Residual Freedom to Operate. This of course is made easier by the first challenge (above) and involves a similar process of starting with the purpose of a given role and considering the variations in how that purpose can be satisfied. An example of this is that of the role of airlines in providing on-board safety briefings. The assumption that they must all accord to precisely the same wording, tone and style would support the view that there was a limited Residual Freedom to Operate. However, examples such as the Southwest Airlines rap and the Cebu Pacific safety dance demonstrate that such limiting assumptions can be challenged and in doing so can lead to better results (see Figure 4.2).

FIGURE 4.2 An illustration of the effect of creatively challenging limiting assumptions about the Absolute and Residual Freedoms to Operate

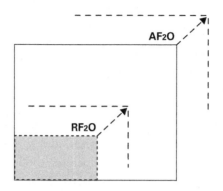

Individual and group level Freedom to Operate

When contemplating and testing the boundaries of the Freedom to Operate it doesn't take long before it is necessary to consider how changes in one area of the business might affect another. And bearing in mind that many people work as part of a team (whether loose, tight, proximate or remote), the exercise of freedoms quickly rubs up against others. And so at a technical level of the relationship between tasks, and at the human level of the relationship between people, there is a need to pause and take on board a broader picture. Traditionally this is firmly within the domain of management. Managers act as coordinators that seek, for understandable reasons, to orchestrate the flow and interconnections of work packages.

Under the Freedoms Model it is not suggested that managers should stop this, but that as they invite their team members to accept greater Freedom to Operate it is necessary that they accordingly embolden them to negotiate the relationships and consequences that arise.

And so we can think of this as being an important part of the obligations that sit with both workers and managers. But because we envisage a workplace design that has workers proactively seeking better solutions to the challenges they face, and at liberty to enact developments and changes, it is important that a dynamic process of 'intelligence gathering' and anticipation is very much part of the employee role.

In the same way that an amateur footballer might begin with particular individual skills that make them an effective footballer, their commitment to improvement increasingly depends on their ability to work within a team. And in doing so they would need to explore how their skill at heading balls in the midfield, for example, might fit with the skill that the goalkeeper has in striking long balls. On this basis the player may choose to position him or herself in midfield when goal kicks are taken or if another player has the same skills then they may revise their approach. Or for that matter they would need to decide whether their ambition to adopt a more offensive strategy accords or could work alongside the strategy, ambition and so on imagined by his team members. As we will explore later in this chapter the need to communicate different perspectives, and to do so often and skilfully becomes much greater when implementing the Freedoms Model. This is examined in the Freedom to Speak section.

A further consideration arising from an awareness of the relationship between individual and group Freedom to Operate relates to the implications for efficiency. As argued by the Six Sigma school of thinking, variations in processes give rise to inefficiency. And with this in mind supporters of the Six Sigma methodology would seek to 'iron out' the variations that would arise from allowing greater Freedom to Operate envisaged in the Freedoms model.

We have two observations to make about the rigorous pursuit of efficiency that is central to Six Sigma and other similar methodologies such as Lean Management and Business Process Re-engineering.

There is a dangerous tension between the aspiration to standardize human processes in order to deliver efficiencies, and the aspiration, as set out in this book, of achieving authenticity at work. The more that people are seen as cogs in a mechanical process, the more that their work is specified by the outcome of Six Sigma reviews and the like, and the more that discretion is removed, the less that people are likely to feel authentic and valued at work. Even though some efficiency-creating processes such as Lean Management are designed to empower workers in the first instance to collectively locate options for efficiency, the outcome will always amount to a reduction in decision-making latitude and a standardization of processes. For these reasons we argue for circumspection in the implementation of efficiency focused initiatives, and invite those in favour of Six Sigma, Lean and so on to consider the human cost in terms of authenticity, as well as the impact on motivation, agility, accountability and so on.

That said, we believe that efficiency should be a 'top-of-the-head' consideration as workers exercise their Freedom to Operate. And as individuals develop their ideas for changing how they work, and as they interact with others in the process, they should factor into their thinking the collective impact of change, or even continuation, on efficiency. But one important difference between the two strategies of: a) following the process prescriptions arising from efficiency-review processes (eg Six Sigma); and b) following the process creations arising from the individual Freedom to Operate is that of where responsibility lies and is felt. Enacting the Freedom to Operate generates personal responsibility in ways that imposed process requirements do not, and arguably, if we want employees to be thinking, as a matter of course, about how work should be undertaken and improvements should be made, then every effort should be made to help them feel in control of their circumstances and responsible for the decisions they make.

Where ideas might come from in exercising the Freedom to Operate

In many organizations, particularly those that have historically favoured a limited individual Freedom to Operate, it may not follow that as greater freedoms are offered workers will either naturally embrace the opportunity, or 'step up' with a full set of ready-made ideas for doing business differently. And this is for good reason as there is a degree of safety to be found in acting in accordance with established norms and management directions, and there may be a fear of the sanctions attracted by exercising greater Freedom to Operate. And so at one level this might be the first barrier that is met under this new approach. However, our view is that if the management climate is right (which we discuss later) much of this understandable reticence can dissipate relatively quickly and inertia can rapidly turn into momentum.

Dimensions of improvement

But there is a separate question worth examining which is where ideas might emerge from in the first instance in determining the direction that freedoms might follow. We first see this question as being posed in the context of an enlarged Absolute Freedom to Operate (AF2O) and an enlarged Residual Freedom to Operate (RF2O). The process alluded to earlier is one that involves creatively challenging limiting assumptions about both parameters. And so this acts as the first spur to generate possibilities.

Beyond this though there are a broad range of provocations and inspirations that can be used. We can think for example of the processes that we follow or even the services that we deliver, and the ways in which we might make these better. Below are 20 dimensions of improvement that are not exhaustive but may nevertheless be helpful in focusing effort on where to exercise the Freedom to Operate. In doing so we ask, how can we make a process or service:

1 Quicker

2 Easier

3 Simpler

4 Deliver more value

5 Be more attractive

6 Cost less

7 More timely

8 More efficient

9 Generate more custom

10 Create more learning

11 Generate more loyalty

12 Beat the competition

13 Engage people more

14 Inspire better collaboration

15 Uphold company values better

16 Utilize technology more effectively

17 Produce better management information

18 Better align with the vision for the organization

19 Remove unnecessary effort

20 Make life easier for others

Whether we are talking about the checkout operator in a supermarket, the casual worker on a building site, the university lecturer, the government policy maker, the creative in an advertising agency, the payroll clerk, the shoe repairer or the police officer walking the beat, these provocations can help remind and inspire each employee about the areas in which they can exercise their Freedom to Operate. And importantly, it is the familiarity of each employee with the task under consideration and their intimate understanding of the prevailing opportunities and difficulties that qualifies them so well to be in the driving seat of making the necessary change. This we say on the understanding that workers too pay attention to the obligations that sit alongside the Freedom to Operate model.

The power of 'reintegrated thinking'

Another rich source of ideas for how to make improvements in a way that sees workers acting on their Freedom to Operate is referred to in earlier work by one of the authors of this book (Ryde, 2007[5]). The particular approach described is in reaction to a dominant mode of thinking called 'Binary Thinking', which allows seemingly opposing positions to be accepted as choices to be made. The word binary is used to convey the 'Either – Or' paradigm that is offered. An example of this in business might be the assumption that we must choose between high quality or low cost goods, or equally a choice between being product or service led, or we choose between centralization and devolution of power. The alternative paradigm to Binary Thinking is what is called 'Reintegrated Thinking' where 'Either – Or' is replaced by the 'Both – And' provocation. Adopting this approach we ask questions such as: Under what circumstances might we deliver both high value quality and at a low cost?; How might we both be product and service led? and What are the possibilities for realizing the benefits of both centralized and devolved power? The reason for offering this way of thinking in the context of the Freedom to Operate is that often people assume that they are confined to one of the two options that the Binary Thinking paradigm creates, and they therefore assume a limited Freedom to Operate.

For example, a checkout operator in a supermarket might assume that while they would like to engage customers in conversation they are limited in doing so because they are under pressure to move quickly through the process to serve the next customer in the queue. A choice is often therefore made. However, with the creative question 'how might I both move through the process quickly, and also take the opportunity to engage properly with customers?' some interesting examples of the Freedom to Operate might be revealed. With this provocation in mind we might think of designating a number of 'no hurry' checkouts. We might designate a small number of 'customer insight' checkouts where customers receive a discount for engaging in conversation about their experience of the store as they pass through the checkout. Or if we focus on the idea that checkouts become too impersonal in the pursuit of speed, then we might consider individualized changes to uniforms or other personalized expressions that don't impact on processing speeds.

Above all though, while we might project priorities or solutions onto a worker in their role, the essence of this approach is that possibilities are generated by the task-owners themselves which we believe not only produces better ideas but also lifts employee engagement with it. The management task acts in support of this; catalysing ideas, disseminating learning, and assisting in aligning effort across the business.

Comparisons near and far

Another inspiration in contemplating opportunities to exercise greater Freedom to Operate is through making comparisons. If we return to our example of the supermarket checkout operator, we have some ready-made points of comparison in the form of multiple identical checkout processes. The queues in some checkouts will move quicker than others, the level of conversation with customers will vary, customers will seem to enjoy the experience to differing degrees and so on. Looking to what appears to be causing these differences will offer clues and hints about what might be explored and experimented with elsewhere. In this example, while the extent of variability may be relatively narrow, comparisons between different practices will nevertheless provide ideas and provocations for workers to enact their Freedom to Operate.

However, possibilities for discovering particularly innovative alternatives may be found by making comparisons to processes or organizations that appear to be much more dissimilar in nature (see Figure 4.3). If we take for example the role of a police officer in walking the beat, a close comparison to draw would be to the practices of other police officers in different locations but we may feel that this may not deliver radical ideas for improvement or change. A much more unusual (and dissimilar) comparison might be to look, for example, to how street performers operate (as both police officers and street performers work on the street, connect with passers-by, form a relationship with people, build trust, want to be noticed and so on). And in making this comparison the police officer may find inspiration, that they hadn't previously considered, for example in:

- Taking steps to attract greater, positive interest from the general public (as the street performer does). Making their appearance on the streets a source of excitement rather than, what may be perceived as, an unwanted presence.

- Being seen in areas where larger groups typically congregate (making their presence known with more people).

- Considering how their appearance might be altered to look less authoritative and more approachable (in the case of the street performer this extends to looking fun and, at times, wacky). In some countries community police dress noticeably differently, and more 'softly', to regular police.

- Walking the streets at predictable times and places (while this might work counter to the idea of taking potential criminals by surprise, it might create greater trust).

In addition to those mentioned, there are a variety of other sources of inspiration that workers might use in guiding their Freedom to Operate, but in most cases ideas to make changes and improvements will derive from the hard-earned experience that workers develop over time.

To illustrate many of the points raised in this section, we look to the example of a successful British company, Timpson, which is known not only for its successful growth strategy during one of the worst recessions in the past century, but also for its commitment to an alternative 'upside down' approach to management.

FIGURE 4.3 A model relating the similarity of comparators and the scope for drawing out innovative lessons

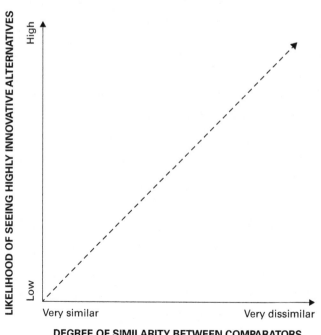

LIKELIHOOD OF SEEING HIGHLY INNOVATIVE ALTERNATIVES

High

Low

Very similar — Very dissimilar

DEGREE OF SIMILARITY BETWEEN COMPARATORS

CASE STUDY   The Freedom to Operate, and more

Background

Timpson is a family owned and run business based in Manchester, UK. Founded in 1865 as a shoe retailer it currently employs over 3,000 people predominantly offering shoe repairs, key cutting, engraving, watch repairs, dry cleaning and photographic development alongside a range of other services through almost 1,000 local branches distributed throughout Ireland and the UK.

'Upside down management'

Chairman John Timpson and CEO James Timpson operate a philosophy that they call 'upside down management': 'Our culture is unique, with the colleagues driving the business being the ones that serve the customers. This is what we call upside down management.'

Although they have arrived at this perspective over many years, and John cites Robert K Greenleaf's *Servant Leadership* as an inspiration, it is possible to observe the Freedom to Operate model in play here. Staff, or 'colleagues', who work at the interface with the customer, are placed at the top of the traditional pyramid and the management at the bottom in a supporting role. Colleagues exercise a surprising level of autonomy at the branch level while managers are required to remove obstacles to allow them the freedom to run the branches in the way that they think offers the best service to customers. The Head Office, called 'HQ Support', is there to offer advice, guidance and support immediately when called upon by the branches:

> I can just pick up the phone and speak to anyone at HQ and they are there to help. (Jordan, trainee)

The Freedom to Operate

The most striking symbol of the level of freedom afforded Timpson colleagues is visible in every branch. Prominently displayed is a sign featuring the Chairman, John Timpson, and the message: 'The staff in this shop have my total authority to do whatever they can to give you amazing service.'

In an organization characterized by plain speaking, this is a perfect articulation of their management strategy. Jay, an Area Manager, told us: 'It's simple, the guys in the stores know best. They're in the stores. They are making the money that pays my wages.'

What does this freedom look like?

Each branch manager is authorized to set prices and promotions, order stock, negotiate reciprocal arrangements with local shops and businesses, trial new stock etc. In fact, Timpson HQ are so committed to their hands-off approach that they do not use Electronic Point of Sale (EPOS) tills in the stores to monitor stock levels and all management information is completed by branches at the end of every working day, by hand, and sent in to HQ. Jay told us: 'Why have endless printouts when you can just ask the guy?'

This discretion extends to dispute resolution where each branch has a budget of up to £500 per single dispute to secure a satisfactory conclusion for customers.

> They can charge what they want, order their own stock, change the displays.
> They can even paint their shop a different colour to make more money – that's
> fine by us.' (James Timpson, CEO)

Employees are encouraged to use their initiative in identifying new business opportunities. For example, one store manager in a branch that we visited located near an Embassy, noticed that he was attracting enquiries about photocopying services. His enquiries revealed that the Embassy had no provision for people to copy documents in support of visa and passport applications. He invested his own funds in a standard copier and pretty soon had recouped his initial investment and was generating a healthy sum towards earning his monthly bonus. Other branches have identified opportunities in their local area striking up arrangements with shoe retailers and sports clubs; they are only limited by their imagination.

Systems are kept deliberately simple, Timpson consistently wins awards for clear communication, in order to allow the maximum space and time for staff to operate. Bonus mechanisms, for example, are clearly communicated and never changed so that the benefit of discretionary effort remains achievable and motivating.

These freedoms extend to non-branch staff, where budgets are managed by individual departments rather than routed through finance or procurement staff.

Obligations

The 'red lines' within which colleagues can operate are very clear, but articulated with a 'min spec' economy (ie a minimum level of specification is preferred). Colleagues must ensure that:

- all money ends up in the till;

- they look presentable and wear a tie;

- they are courteous to customers; and

- they work to the best of their ability.

These standards are reiterated throughout the organization in training material, guidance booklets, posters and a whole raft of methods in order to communicate the message in ways most accessible to all Timpson staff.

Everyone is required to work at the highest level to a '9 or 10' assessment score. This is accompanied by a 'no drongoes' policy in place from recruitment onwards. Area managers routinely circulate the stores in their area, giving face-to-face attention to colleagues. Jay visited most branches under his responsibility each week and knew the name and abilities of everyone. This level of contact creates awareness of impending performance issues that are dealt with in Timpson in a no-nonsense and decisive way. The ethos is that people working at full capacity do not deserve to be saddled with underperforming co-workers, and if remedial action does not work, then colleagues are not encouraged to stay within the organization.

Area managers use their close knowledge of their colleagues to design motivational interventions too. Fun is encouraged and rewards are personalized. For example we saw that a relatively new member of staff had been given tickets to see his favourite football team in return for his commitment. And another colleague received a handwritten letter from James Timpson praising him for good work.

In order to exercise their freedom to the best effect, Timpson staff are required to develop an intimate knowledge of the company. Every person that we spoke to, even the trainees, knew the best performing colleagues in their area, the targets that they had to meet, the newest stores.

Timpson staff are in no doubt about their purpose and HQ has a model store set up in reception to remind people that they are there to support the core business.

Trust

The freedoms extended to Timpson staff stem largely from the trust that can be afforded to people who are willing to give their best and James Timpson makes it that they recruit on personality and motivation rather than academic achievement or previous experience. In his mind it is a simple case of: 'Get bloody good people, and let them get on with it.'

Conversely, since there is no anxiety around hanging on to poor performing staff, those who remain are trusted and supported in work to provide excellent customer service.

A sense of trust flows like a lifeblood through the business, from the lack of sign-off and surveillance procedures, such as EPOS tills, to the accessibility of information about the fortunes of the company. Face-to-face contact is highly valued as a way to build trust and John and James Timpson devote much of their time to meeting every member of staff in person.

Staff are encouraged to think of themselves as a family, engaged in mutually aiding each other to achieve success. First name terms are used and colleagues do not deal with faceless departments. Flexible working and benevolent schemes, such as the hardship fund, also foster trust and commitment and in James's view, if people are willing to do their best for Timpson, then the organization must equal that by doing its best to support them in their lives outside of work. Likewise, managers are recruited from within, emphasizing the message that hard work and loyalty are rewarded.

Timpson works hard to demonstrate that they value their employees. Everyone gets a day off on their birthday, they can take advantage of free holiday homes, and an extra week of paid leave for their honeymoon, and can enjoys bbqs and events at the Timpson family home.

Learning

With such a high level of personal contact, it is no surprise that innovations and best practice is transmitted across the organization largely by the area managers who share this information freely and widely. The area managers also help to interpret and frame the values of the business. One area manager explains: 'Everything we sell is a grudge purchase, no one wants to be here, so we try to make it a pleasant experience.'

Colleagues circulate between branches and are exposed to the various systems and cultures that they encounter. Although most learning is experiential, there are a wide range of simple and direct booklets, setting out the story and values of Timpson, describing the routes available to promotion and advancement; and setting out the benefits available to established staff.

The CEO explains how colleagues in branches are essential to creating new business models. In 2013, Timpson had acquired a high street photographic company and were engaged in adapting the stores to the Timpson model. James Timpson described how the branches were turned over to the staff to determine the best way to leverage the business and report back their findings until a consistent approach could be determined. This ground-up approach is entirely consistent with the upside down model.

Benefits

At a time of world economic recession, Timpson has enjoyed growth and profitability alongside a strong reputation for quality of service. James Timpson is convinced that this success can be attributed to the level of discretion that his staff can employ in the service of customers. We see branches that can reflect and respond to the requirements of their location and the individual needs of their customers demonstrating high levels of agility. Information and learning is constantly shared and services honed. A loyal workforce with low churn retains experience and internalizes the values of the organization.

However, one of the most striking benefits is seen in the level of pride and happiness in the people employed by the company. Timpson take this very seriously. Jordan, a young trainee, put it well when he described how: 'Working here is a laugh, if I'm not doing anything on the weekend, I like coming into work... Yes, I'm ambitious, I wasn't until I got here, now I want to really get on.'

Interviews and observations took place between July and August 2013

Key questions to help develop your Freedom to Operate (F2O)

1 What are the limiting assumptions relating to your organization's Absolute Freedom to Operate (AF2O), and how might these be creatively challenged?

2 What are the limiting assumptions relating to your role and the Residual Freedom to Operate (RF2O), and how might these be creatively challenged?

3 Assuming that you have the opportunity and backing to broaden your Freedom to Operate, what would be the candidate areas where you would seek to make changes?

4 Which of the (20) dimensions of improvement identified earlier might offer the greatest inspiration?

5 In relation to the candidate areas for development, what kind of research, exploration or experimentation would need to take place to advance your ideas?

6 Which areas and people in particular are most likely to be impacted by the developments and changes you might want to make?

7 Which of the following obligations in particular might you need to work on?:

– the obligation to engage with the corporate messages and priorities of the organization so that freedoms are taken in full awareness of these;
– the obligation to honour the ethics and values of the organization when acting on freedoms;
– the obligation to proactively share the success or otherwise of acting on the freedoms;
– the obligation to undertake 'de-risking' activity when attempting new and novel approaches;
– the obligation to build understanding (and act on this) of the potential impact of changes and actions arising from freedoms; and
– the obligation to accept accountability for actions that arise from accepting freedoms.

8 As you consider exercising your Freedom to Operate, notice how this impacts upon your own sense of your authenticity at work.

9 Notice too the contribution that greater Freedom to Operate makes to your happiness at work.

Notes

1 Job Control in Britain: Skills and Employment Survey 2012.
2 These ideas are referred to in and throughout the work of Daniel Pink and David McClelland, and the core texts where they are articulated are: Pink, DH (2011) *Drive: The Surprising Truth About What Motivates Us*, Cannongate Books; McClelland, DC (1987) *Human Motivation*, Cambridge University Press.
3 Chartered Institute of Personnel Development (2012) Are Organisations Losing the Trust of their Workers?
4 Kirschenbaum, H and Henderson, VL (eds) (1989) *The Carl Rogers Reader: Selections from the lifetime work of America's preeminent psychologist, author of* On Becoming a Person *and* A Way of Being, Houghton Mifflin Harcourt.
5 Ryde, R (2007) *Thought Leadership: Moving hearts and minds*, Palgrave Macmillan.

The second freedom
The Freedom to Speak

05

Don't you see that the whole aim of Newspeak is to narrow the range of thought? In the end we shall make thought-crime literally impossible, because there will be no words in which to express it. Every concept that can ever be needed will be expressed by exactly one word, with its meaning rigidly defined and all its subsidiary meanings rubbed out and forgotten... The process will still be continuing long after you and I are dead. Every year fewer and fewer words, and the range of consciousness always a little smaller... Has it ever occurred to you, Winston, that by the year 2050, at the very latest, not a single human being will be alive who could understand such a conversation as we are having now?[1]

GEORGE ORWELL, *NINETEEN EIGHTY-FOUR*

The Freedom to Speak (F2S) identified as the second element to the Freedoms Model carries a more expansive meaning than it might appear on first reading. While this is about the importance of employees being able to articulate their views, ideas, feelings, hopes and concerns within the organization, and all of this happening without censorship or constraint, it is also a strong encouragement for this to happen often, and to deep level. Rather than the narrow range of thoughts, words and debate implied by the situation in Orwell's *Nineteen Eighty-Four*, we propose the Freedom to Speak as an invitation to broaden the range of thoughts, words and debate at large within the organization.

FIGURE 5.1a The office environment of the past!

SOURCE Shutterstock/Everett Collection.

FIGURE 5.1b Children sitting at their school desks in a classroom doing scholarship examinations, 16 April 1940

SOURCE Author unknown; photo from John Oxley Library, State Library of Queensland.

The black and white films and photographs of the office environment of the 1940s, 50s and 60s (see Figure 5.1a) give an indication of the attitude that was taken towards discussion and dialogue between employees in the workplace. The office scene of the time frequently depicts employees as sitting in separate, ordered and clearly demarcated rows, amid an atmosphere of almost total silence; a design and an environment not dissimilar to that

FIGURE 5.2 Four-box diagram to illustrate the aspiration of achieving both a high volume/amount of dialogue and a high quality of dialogue in the organization

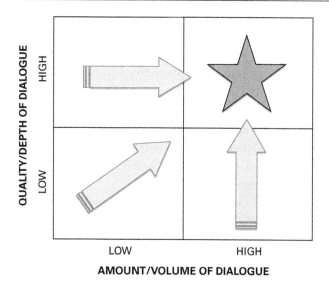

found in the school examination hall of the same period (see Figure 5.1b). For many years in the workplace, productivity and efficiency have been closely associated with the idea of 'getting your head down' and quietly 'getting on with the job'. In fact to engage in conversation that wasn't demonstrably essential to the task at hand, was to breach the implicit terms of employment. Put simply, talking, more often than not, got in the way of the job.

Our proposal, as a part of the Freedoms Model, is that talking is as much as a part of the job as the 'doing' bit. And not only is the volume important but the quality and depth of conversation too. The diagram in Figure 5.2 illustrates the importance of these two elements together and the desired direction of travel.

Talk and the intended domain of value creation (IDVC)

Modern organizations are thankfully not as quiet as the exam halls or the offices of the mid-20th century. Dialogue is a staple component of modern working and although we can still witness the cubiform design of some workplaces, and we can still see the remnants of the desire to order, to separate and to monitor the conduct of workers, it is clear that times have changed. However, it is because of this very reason – that we live in different circumstances – that the need to step up the quantity and quality of conversation comes into sharp focus.

In the previous chapter we spoke of the 'slushy' environment in which we live – one where the pace of change causes us to be 'caught out' and leave unfinished our plans to re-shape (or re-freeze) our businesses to keep pace. Others have referred to the modern context as one that is volatile, uncertain, complex and ambiguous (called VUCA). Agility and adaptability become the new idols of the modern operating context. Organizations that aren't able to anticipate fluctuations, quickly make sense of what is going on, be agile, adapt and so on, run the risk of being beaten by the competition and pushed out of business.

During the global financial crisis many previously successful businesses found themselves filing for bankruptcy, asking for bailouts from the government, or otherwise having to radically reappraise their operations. In the UK for example, companies like HMV (music and video retailer) faced the prospect of extinction and their future still hangs in the balance, while familiar high street stores such as Woolworths simply vanished out of sight. In November 2008, Woolworths plc went into administration taking with it 800 stores across the country and 27,000 jobs. This happened when the company was just a few months away from its 100-year anniversary. In the United States, stores like Borders fell into administration during the global financial crisis, and American Airlines (as part of the AMR parent corporation) had to be rescued by the US government. This was the second time that it closely avoided bankruptcy, the first being in the wake of the 9/11 terrorist attacks. The list however continues with a host of other national and global companies fighting for their lives and many of them failing including Kodak, Blockbuster, General Motors, Lehman Brothers, Clinton Cards, Readers Digest, Sea France, Habitat, Comet, Jessops and so the list goes on.

The operating environment moves and undulates in ways, and at a pace, that many find hard to keep up with. It is for this reason that organizations need to be able to see and recognize the changes that are occurring, to subject them to analysis and to rapidly generate options to deal with them. And this applies as much to threats as it does to opportunities. Dialogue is the engine that drives this process and it has to be a process that is not simply the preserve of the most senior in the enterprise. Unfortunately, we have seen this movie play out before, and leaving the decision-making to those at the top does not guarantee the survival of the corporation, nor does it always lead to the kind of ethical behaviour that we would hope to see being demonstrated. In the shifting landscape of business, public management and so on we need all eyes on the scene, with situation reports, perspectives and analyses forthcoming from all levels.

Talk more generally though can take many forms, and it is helpful at this point to introduce the concept of the Intended Domain of Value Creation (IDVC) to explore this. The IDVC refers to the intended benefit and the intended beneficiary of all organizational dialogue. The starting point is that in all conversation those holding and contributing to the dialogue will have the intention to create value in some way, even if this is only to be self-serving, eg to offload worries about the latest corporate initiative. There are seven key domains where value might be delivered through organizational discourse. This is not an exhaustive list of domains but offers a sense of the areas commonly receiving attention, and standing to gain benefit, namely:

1 the self;

2 colleagues;

3 clients;

4 partners (including suppliers, contractors, etc);

5 processes/systems;

6 the task at hand; and

7 organization, eg relating to the next major corporate initiative, organizational ethics, fitness to deliver etc.

Ultimately though, we can reduce the divisions apparent here in terms of the IDVC to just two, that is the organizational domain (the organization being the intended beneficiary of value), and the personal domain (the individual being the intended beneficiary of value). And in the same sense, we can conceive of conversations of this sort as occurring in two 'spaces', namely a formal space, eg business meetings, and in an informal space, eg chatting at the coffee point. Figure 5.3 illustrates this distinction.

Under the Freedom to Speak, as explained earlier, our aim here first and foremost is to increase the volume and quality of dialogue in all four quadrants. Strategies for overcoming the barriers and limitations of each are discussed later, but in the meantime it is important to acknowledge the benefits to be found in each arena, and the particular qualities that belong to each:

- Formal and organizational dialogue: it is in the formal space where much of the organizational-level dialogue often occurs. The benefit of formality in this domain of intended value creation (ie the organization) is that the content of discussion is typically officially recognized, it may be recorded (eg minutes), it can offer an 'audit trail' of decision-making, and it will often accord to appropriate conventions (eg the right people needing to be present at meetings for decisions to be ratified). Dialogue in this space is undertaken explicitly in the interests of the organization and so challenges to the organization (like those referred to earlier in relation to the global financial crisis for example) and opportunities (for example those associated with developing technology) will be dealt with here. However, it is significant that many of the protocols and conventions associated with the formal space can make it difficult for free-ranging and diverse conversation to take place. Furthermore, formal dialogue is often codified and mired in corporate and technical language that can, at times, advance exploration, but also can lock people into patterns of thinking and limit the ability to see the unusual, and to see ideas that fall outside the frame of discussion. Events such as the global financial crisis very much fall into the realm of the unusual.

FIGURE 5.3 Four-box matrix illustrating the intended domain of value creation (IDVC) against the 'space' in which dialogue occurs

		FORMAL	INFORMAL
INTENDED DOMAIN OF VALUE CREATION	**ORGANIZATIONAL**	Example Discussing budgets, at a monthly project review	Example Talking about the new structure, over lunch
	PERSONAL	Example Requesting a training opportunity, in a performance appraisal meeting	Example Talking about the journey to work, at the water cooler

CONVERSATIONAL 'SPACE'

- Formal and personal dialogue: conversations taking place in the formal domain and focused on personal considerations (in the example given of a discussion about training opportunities arising in a performance appraisal discussion), attract the same formal qualities as before (having appropriate conventions, being officially recognized etc) but are undertaken principally in the interests of the individual. And while this might seem to be of lesser importance than explicitly creating value to the organization, in the context of seeking greater authenticity in the workplace, this is an important activity. It is in this space that questions might be posed about the level of engagement in the work, the meaning that work carries, the enjoyment that is derived and so on. But as with the previous category, the formal nature of the conversation may make it difficult to get underneath the issues being discussed, or to say things that, while being important, an individual might not want to 'go on the record'. Furthermore, there may be difficulty in framing personal discussions in a vernacular that is formulated for business. This can be a serious limitation to this mode of dialogue.

- Informal and organizational dialogue: the discussion of organizational issues in an informal space is a fascinating topic, not least because the constraints that are present in a formal space are largely absent here, and we can infer that in speaking 'off the record' conversation stands a better chance of being honest, authentic and free-ranging (although this is not a guarantee). During change for example, leaders are likely to gain valuable insights into the 'real' reactions and intentions of workers if they are able to step out of the formal space, and hold informal dialogue. And what may be regarded as unsayable in the formal space (we refer here also to the notion of the 'elephant in the room') will routinely be discussable in the informal space. For example, with organizations that have faced threats from the skilful use of technologically by competitors (for example the threat that Amazon posed to Borders) it is often in the informal spaces where recognition of this can first bubble up, and where creative solutions can be found. However, it is when the content of these conversations does not leap from the informal into the formal realm that opportunities to take coordinated action may be lost. We may also find that much of the conversation in the informal space, while reflecting an interest in the organization itself, is critical in tone and an expression of complaint of one sort or another. And in this way it acts more as a cathartic release, than a constructive contribution to organizational well-being.

- Informal and personal dialogue: at one level, we might see informal dialogue that is focused on the individual interests of those involved as nothing more than chatter, background conversation or 'small talk', and not a topic that warrants serious attention. However, beyond even the value of this kind of dialogue in terms of its contribution to relationship building, networking and so on, it is a truly important space where sense making occurs. And the sense making that goes on through informal exchanges, can relate to almost any topic that is thrown up by the work environment. In contrast with the formal arena, it will provide perhaps the only space where honest and undiluted discussion can take place about what it means to work in the organization. And because it is focused on the personal it is here that we will learn how people feel about their work, what values are being enacted, what fears are at large, what meaning people give to their work, how stretched people feel, whether people are happy, what they treat as unsayable in the formal arena.

To summarize the intent of the Freedom to Speak (F2S) component of the model, we propose that workers are both encouraged to, and take up opportunities to:

- speak freely and often, about their views and ideas (turn up the volume of dialogue);
- talk about their views and ideas in a way that is honest, authentic and at a deep level (raise the quality of dialogue);
- discuss issues relating to the meaning and value of the work they do, and their ability to be authentic in the workplace (leverage the benefits of the personal domain);
- discuss issues relating to organizational well-being, particularly where they are picking up data and signs relating to opportunities or threats (leverage the benefits of the organizational domain);
- ensure that important information, ideas and perspectives make the leap from the informal arena into the formal realm; and
- make nothing unsayable (within reason) in the formal space. Name and discuss the 'elephant in the room' – it may be the most valuable contribution you can make.

Releasing the benefits of the Freedom to Speak

The management task remains an important ally in delivering the benefits of the Freedoms model and the Freedom to Speak (discussed later), but there are other important considerations to explore in order to fully leverage the benefits available. We can look at these in the following ways:

- reducing deference within the organization;
- removing a 'parent–child' mindset from the organization;
- reducing 'deficit thinking' in the organization;
- minimizing technical and corporate language that excludes and disables conversation;
- bringing background issues into the foreground of conversation;
- the value of discourse across multiple fora and platforms; and
- the opportunity offered by everyday conversational tools and techniques.

Reducing deference within the organization

The word 'deferential' can be traced back to Latin, comprising two parts – 'de' which means *down*, and 'ferrere' which means *carry*, which taken together refer to the act of carrying oneself down, or bowing down, to authority. For the purposes of this discussion, deference refers to a behaviour of automatically yielding or submitting to the wishes, judgements or rulings of 'superiors'. Words associated with this process include acquiescence, compliance, obedience, biddability and submission. It is our view that most organizations operate through systems of deference and that this has an unwelcome impact on the Freedom to Speak, on authenticity, but also in other regards.

For organizations, the fundamental problem with systems of deference is that they cause a drag on organizational performance and on the ability to change. The context for organizations is relevant in considering the contribution of deference.

The modern operating context is one that is characterized by volatility, uncertainty, complexity and ambiguity; we see this with technological change, economic shifts, generational factors, interdependence between systems (for example, banking systems), environmental pressures and so on, all of which place a requirement on organizations to be agile and responsive; if nothing else, to keep up. For many years we have talked about this environment but never before has it been so palpably real, and never before has the ambition to survive and thrive depended so much on agility, pace and inventiveness.

The core problem with systems of deference is that they serve to block many of the essential ingredients required to succeed in these circumstances. Deference stands in our way, rather than facilitating the right organizational response.

Systems of deference create 'them and us' cultures; they divide rather than unite organizations, and importantly they quieten the voices of the deferrers in ways that cause employees to refrain from offering their ideas, their discretionary effort and their emotional commitment. The diversity of voices, ideas and solutions that might otherwise flow through the organizational system become muted and in their place can be found a narrow band of judgements asserted by the most deferred to in the organization. The more deference there is, the narrower the band of judgements on which organizations rely. Deference acts like the fatty deposits that build up in arteries; restricting the flow of fresh, oxygen enriched blood across the system.

By concentrating decision-making power, authority and responsibility in the hands of the deferred to, as we witness in so many organizations, the opportunities for broadening and sharing responsibility are significantly reduced. In deferential organizations when the leaders of the organizations stand up and announce the next big thing, the workers smile and wish them good luck, very often not feeling it is their (the workers') responsibility. In short, they don't say what they mean, anticipating that a more honest response would be unwelcome.

So it is no surprise during times of change that deference drives acquiescence to the new ways of operating called for by the deferred to, but it does not drive authentic dialogue or commitment to change. As such we see a behaviour best described as 'consent and evade', where employees seeking to avoid challenge or unwelcome scrutiny from the deferred to, give indications of their consent for change, but ultimately evade it. A bit like the teenager that is told to wash their hands before dinner only to go upstairs and run the water in the hand basin for as long as it would take, without their hands once getting wet – that's consent and evade, and that's what systems of deference cause.

And as for governance and ethical business, systems of deference have for far too long enabled critical and influential decisions to remain unchecked and unchallenged because the decision-makers are treated with high levels of deference. From examples ranging from Enron/Andersen to the Global Financial Crisis to the UK Members of Parliament expenses scandal to the fascinating instance of the CEO of an Indian company that literally invented thousands of non-existent employees to strengthen the company's figures, we see how deference insulates decision-makers against appropriate challenge.

And so deference becomes a seriously limiting factor in the ability of organizations to hear different perspectives (at least to those of the 'deferred to'), and to enable employees to engage in real, authentic, meaningful discussion. Deference constrains the Freedom to Speak and as such needs to be reduced as much as possible. In its place, incidentally, we are not proposing an absence of respect between people and levels, as this remains a fundamental human obligation. But we are proposing action to bring about a reduction in deference. One particular model that can be useful in combatting deference, offered previously by one of the authors of this book,[2] is called the SPEED model (Figure 5.4). Let us offer a short summary of the possibilities that face use.

Working through the model in a clockwise direction, we start with symbols. Symbols tell us a lot about attitudes to deference and they are there in front of us, at work, everyday. Organizations signal their support for deference in different ways; ranging from terms of address to communication rituals to the amount of office space afforded to the 'deferred to'. In some organizations it might be the express elevator reserved for the senior managers that will provides us with clues. In other settings it will be the extent to which access to individuals is enabled or constrained by physical location or 'protective' assistants. Signs and symbols are highly observable and are an

FIGURE 5.4 The SPEED model used to reduce deference within organizations

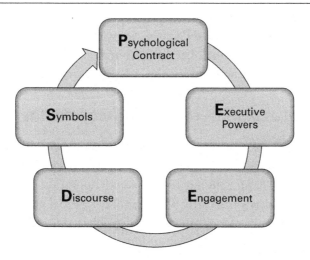

excellent place to start in the hunt for deference. The encouragement here is first to become mindful of the symbols in the organization and for people, at all levels, to remove them. This is not a task that sits only with the leaders and managers in the organizations but symbols of deference can be found at almost every level, the opportunity is there for all to take action.

The second option for reducing deference relates to the psychological contract that exists between workers and managers and the encouragement here is for people, on both sides of the relationship, to ensure that the 'deal' is discussed and that there is integrity in the agreement. For example, we look here to ensure that what managers ask of workers, for example frank and fearless opinions, contribution to organizational change, innovation and creativity (all of these are common espousals by management), is genuinely what is sought. In examining and revealing what is contained in the psychological contract we are asking for a new level of honesty and respect.

Turning to the first 'E' of executive powers the proposition here is to make a shift towards a broader distribution of power. In short, for management to push power down, and for workers to step up and take responsibility. This needs to be done thoughtfully and the game plan should be one of creating a safe transition whereby 'seniors' feel confident and assured as power is shared across the system, and 'juniors' feel as confident and inspired to take on greater levels of responsibility.

The second 'E' of engagement is simply a call for more employee engagement. This is a request that is addressed as much to leaders and managers as it is to workers. We are looking for connection between people, rather than separation. And finally, we see Discourse and conversation needing to happen more often and to a deeper level than is found in most organizations. More on this later.

So, an important catalyst in the process of introducing greater Freedom to Speak, is to begin to dismantle deference within cultures. There are many other benefits that arise in doing this, but in the pursuit of the Freedom to Speak and workplace authenticity, this is a perfect way to make headway.

Removing a 'parent–child' mindset from the organization

A second encouragement is to inspire a shift in discourse away from what psychiatrist Eric Berne calls a parent–child relationship to an adult-to-adult relationship. This is particularly pertinent to deferential cultures previously discussed, which are more likely to cast the 'deferred to' and the 'deferrers' respectively in a parent–child relationship.

In doing so the 'deferred to', acting as the parent, will find themselves adopting a range of behaviours that communicate and reinforce their role. These behaviours may include setting out expectations for others in the organization, exercising power by judging their performance (giving 'feedback'), using powerful and directive language, and through the ability to lead and control conversations. In a slightly different vein, they may at times seek to be over-protective towards the 'deferrers' and in doing so to take away their responsibility (while this may have a positive intent it is easy to seeing the downside of this strategy).

The 'deferrers', acting as the child, may remain silent until spoken to, or until they are invited to contribute. They may show signs of resentment when they feel that they have to comply with decisions that have been made for them. They may find that they publicly agree to what is suggested, while internally having little or no intention to follow through. 'Deferrers', cast in the child role, may also say what they think the 'deferred to' want to hear even though they actually think something very different.

The major problem in all of this is that in the parent or the child mode, positions are taken and the scope for movement on a given issue is severely reduced. And as the role is played out, each party feels increasingly justified in talking and holding onto their position. Eric Berne wrote about the 'games that people play' and we can see here the ways in which roles are taken and repeated, habits are then formed, and cultural norms are created.

The shift that is needed is towards an adult-to-adult dialogue, which is characteristically:

- direct (rather than ambiguous or implied);
- on the same level (as peers might talk);
- transparent (without hidden agendas or inauthenticity); and
- reasoned (reflecting measured thought) and made available to reasoned analysis.

Fortunately, if either side of the relationship commit to breaking out of their mode (parent or child) then a space can open up for the other party to shift their position. In this way power to break the cycle and make a positive change sits with both managers and workers.

Reducing 'deficit thinking' in the organization

'Deficit thinking' is an incredibly powerful mode of thinking. At its most basic level it reflects an instinct to detect danger, to secure our own survival.

But it is applied in a whole range of extreme and less extreme, day-to-day settings. Every time we evaluate something we need to understand where the weaknesses lie, what too are the risks. Picking a good builder needs an eye for unreliability or untidiness. Interviewing applicants for a job needs an eye for incompetence or untrustworthiness. Listening to a sales pitch needs an ear for dishonesty or important omissions. In each and every case what we are using is deficit thinking.

Deficit thinking is characterized by the tendency to anticipate and search out flaws, weaknesses and deficits in what people say, do and write. The language that we have to articulate deficits is abundant. If there are a hundred ways to say 'I love you', there are a thousand ways to say 'you're wrong'. Think of the words – risk, concern, weakness, flaw, gap, inconsistency, error, fault, deficiency, lacking, problem, issue, difficulty, doubt etc – all are there to articulate the identification of fault.

But the term deficit 'thinking' implies more forethought than is actually the case. Better descriptions might be about the impulse to find deficits, the habit of finding flaws, or the reflex to highlight risks. Thinking, very often, doesn't enter into it. And of course the finest, most commonplace and gold-medal-winning words that convey deficit thinking is 'yes, but...' Think of your task for today, or in your next couple of meetings, as being to count the number of times any of these words are used and the number of times people highlight the errors of someone else's thinking, writing, decisions or behaviour. You will see that it's like a virus.

And the reaction to this is worth contemplating, particularly in the context of the Freedom to Speak. In the late 1980s and early 1990s, Chris Argyris introduced the concept of 'defensive routines' and talked about how well meaning people create defensive strategies to avoid threat, embarrassment and negative surprises. Those well-meaning people are, of course, us, and in our daily working lives we do this by a range of approaches such as deploying technical language to fend off challenges, asserting dominance over others, presenting our views as facts, shifting blame, saving face, keeping quiet, self-censoring our comments and so on. Each time we follow such a routine, we distract our attention away from the need to reflect or learn from that situation and we simultaneously get better at being defensive. We also very often take the decision to remove from much of what we say words or ideas that might invite criticism or attack.

Importantly much of the effort involved in defensive routines is triggered by the anticipation or *actualité* of deficit thinking. Our ability to engage in authentic, direct, adult-to-adult conversation is significantly hampered by the presence of deficit thinking and within organizational life, there is a strong argument to look to other ways to add depth to the debate.

Strength-based thinking is one such example. It is a vastly under-used mode of thinking and accounts for a small minority of thinking and dialogue in practice. It denotes a search for strength, for what works well in any given situation, and it provides us with some of the best data available on how problems can be solved and changes can be made. If we are looking for solutions it flags up what we need to hang on to. If we are an organization undergoing change it points to the baby that we don't want to throw out with the bathwater. If we are an organization that is successful it is a style of thinking that leads us to why. In seeing the value in what we do and how we do it, we can think about how it can be multiplied and how it can be better leveraged. In the context of the Freedom to Speak, strength-based thinking injects energy into thinking conversations and builds the confidence of those involved. It is much less likely to trigger defensive routines and is an asset in starting to release a more diverse and deeper dialogue within the organization.

The broader point to be made is that there are very many options for how issues can be framed, and just as many modes of thinking that we might enter into. The key is to adopt approaches that open up dialogue (rather than close down options or people). While this does not guarantee a greater volume and a higher quality of conversation, the more this becomes a cultural norm, the better chance we stand of also making high quality discourse an everyday occurrence.

Minimizing technical and corporate language that excludes and disables conversation

Technical and corporate language is undoubtedly an asset in the business of discourse and useful to us in a number of ways including the advantage of being able to convey complex ideas quickly. Furthermore, we find that the words, expressions and ideas captured by technical and corporate language convey not only the surface sense of what is being articulated but also often a deeper set of the propositions and the history that goes with it. So for example, 'Lean Management' or 'Six Sigma' – both examples of corporate language, and a particular set of methodologies for focusing on efficiency – implicitly refer to the management ideas developed by Frederick Taylor in the early 1900s, the work of W Edwards Deming in the mid 1900s and the manufacturing innovations that helped Japan to achieve the economic dominance that it held for much of the second half of the 20th century.

Contained within these few, short words, is a wealth of meaning that is quite some distance away from the often shallow and modish reputation that corporate (and technical) phraseology is given. In short, the quality of discourse that arises from this form of language can be invaluable to organizational success, and without it most organizations would be much worse off. But all of this depends on four factors:

- That the sender and the receiver share a similar level of understanding about the terms used and the concepts referred to.

- That the intent behind the decision to use corporate/technical language is to bring value to the issue at hand, rather than to claim or assert power, or as a means for the sender to assert superiority.

- That the words, expressions and language used, do not serve to constrain the thinking and imagination of those involved. The example of George Orwell's *Nineteen Eighty-Four* argues this point by suggesting that as a particular set of speech conventions apply, this alters the ability of people to think outside of the language available – 'Every concept that can ever be needed will be expressed by exactly one word, with its meaning rigidly defined and all its subsidiary meanings rubbed out and forgotten.'

- That the use of such language is not in fact a defensive routine.

Our first recommendation therefore is that in order to leverage the benefits of the Freedom to Speak, we urge mindfulness for all those involved regarding the significant risks associated with an improper application of corporate and technical language (as illustrated above). And to be clear, the risks are that their improper use will generate a lower quality of dialogue in the organization and will most likely reduce the volume of dialogue, as people feel inclined to disengage as a result. I remember, many years ago, working with a Defence Agency and engaging in entire conversations without understanding a single word that was said. Of course I nodded and smiled politely as tumbleweeds blew inside my head and acronyms, abbreviations, ranks, security levels and protocols sailed past my ears. I had been skillfully warned off the territory. The defensive routine had been enacted successfully and the impact on conversation was to remove the conversation almost in its entirety – leaving nothing more than a monologue. This is what can be created through the improper use of corporate and technical language.

But, while we may be able to moderate and manage our own use of corporate and technical language, there remains the prospect that others won't, and we see three useful options should such a situation arise:

1 Challenge and request explanation. This may include asking for examples, metaphors and illustrations (the 'what would that look like in practice?' question). The mindset that you carry into this is important and should be one of confident curiosity (confidence, rather than feeling stupid for having asked in the first instance, and curiosity, so your enquiry is genuinely about understanding and not point proving).

2 Don't feel obliged to adopt the speech patterns/language/frame of the other person using technical/corporate jargon. Use the language that you feel most comfortable with.

3 Seek to alter the setting in which conversations take place (to prevent people falling into habits). This might include using formal or informal spaces, and within each category taking the effort to find spaces that free up thinking (and language) rather than encourage 'business as usual'.

Bringing background issues into the foreground of conversation

Chris Argyris talked about this in relation to the 'shadowside'. Robert Kegan and Lisa Lahey talk about this in the context of an 'immunity to change'. Ronald Heifetz approaches this by asking 'what are the realities that we are not facing?' Chris Rodgers describes this as the 'hidden dynamics of change'. Paul Porteous describes this as the difference between what is in the foreground and what sits in the background.

What all of these perspectives share in common is a recognition of the supreme importance of the real, and usually hidden, world of interaction within organizations that very often 'never sees the light of day'. In this context, much of what is *really going on* in the organization is suppressed in favour of an alternative, often more palatable, notion of organizational life. For example, during the Libor (London Interbank Offered Rate) crisis a number of banks were involved in illegally fixing inter-bank lending rates (and many were fined in the order of hundreds of millions of pounds/dollars for doing so). This was an activity that reflected the reality of operating within some banks but, by and large, it was not discussed nor was it acknowledged formally within the organization. A report by an anonymous trader taken from the *Telegraph* at the time (July 2012) illustrates this point that while the reality may be understood it remains out of view:

> The bank could not be seen to be borrowing at high rates, so we were putting in low Libor submissions. The British Bankers' Association [...] asked for a rate submission but there were no checks [...] you lowered the price a few basis points each day. Everyone knew and everyone was doing it.[3]

At the time the UK's Financial Services Agency reported on the scandal illuminating that not only was it widespread but also it had been in effect for many years prior to the discovery:

> On numerous occasions between January 2005 and June 2009, Barclays' Derivatives Traders made requests to its Submitters for submissions based on their trading positions... The misconduct involving internal requests to the Submitters at Barclays was widespread, cutting across several currencies and occurring over a number of years.[4]

It is clear from this report that Barclays was not an isolated protagonist. In addition to the $420 million fine that Barclays Bank plc received, other institutions that were fined for this included UBS ($1.5 billion fine), Royal Bank of Scotland (€260 million), Deutsche Bank (€259 million), JPMorgan (€80 million), and Citigroup (€70 million).

This illustrates the point that the formal and espoused account of organizational life is often different from the reality. And importantly, it is the reality that needs to be brought into the formal realm (or the 'foreground') for action to be taken. The mechanism by which this happens is twofold:

- Firstly, reflective conversations need to take place about what is (really) going on.
- Secondly, for these conversations to be moved from the background/ the informal space to the foreground/the formal space.

It is important to bear in mind that although Libor is a dramatic example of a more negative facet of the background to organizational life, reflective discussions of this sort are needed as much in relation to possibilities as they are to risks.

The sort of topics that might be explored in doing this include:

- shifts in the external environment (eg changes in customer expectations, shifts in media opinion, technological developments, political changes and so on);
- the behaviour and values of partners, suppliers, contracted-out functions etc;

- organizational culture (the norms which reflect 'the way business is done around here');

- working climate (what it feels like for workers to come to, and experience, work);

- the 'psychological contract' (the implicit 'deal' that exists between 'workers' and 'managers');

- competing commitments and values (understanding what tensions exist and how trade-offs are made);

- assumptions (eg about how work *has* to be done, about which results are important, about where there is agreement/disagreement etc); and

- apparent contradictions between what is espoused and what is lived (eg values, behaviour etc).

The process of holding reflective conversations of this sort can be helped enormously by some of the ideals explored earlier in this chapter such as a reduction of workplace deference, adopting an adult-to-adult dialogue, by avoiding the use of deficit language and so on. But ultimately, this approach involves a willingness to vocalize difficult questions and ones to which you don't know the answer.

But it is more than this. The social psychologist Jonathan Haidt brings us an interesting analogy in the form of the 'elephant and the rider', which he uses to illustrate the difference between controlled and automatic processes. Haidt says that our emotional side is represented by the elephant, with our rational side represented by the rider. Perched on top of the elephant is the rider who holds the reins and in every sense appears to be the leader. But the rider's control is always fragile because the rider is so small relative to the elephant. At any time if the six-tonne elephant and the rider disagree about which direction to go, the rider will lose. But this does not distract from the point that the elephant and the rider live in tension with one another. The rider offers rationalization for what is going on, whereas the elephant hints at deeper, more subconscious motivations and impulses. The elephant's search for instant gratification is matched by the rider's orientation to over analyse. The elephant's sheer power and strength is matched by the rider's ability to think and plan beyond the moment.

And this tension can sometimes generate curious results. Take, for example, the scenario of an elderly person who does not use the internet to undertake online banking. If you asked them why this was, the answer (from the rider) that might be given is that they worry that it is insecure, and that this is enough to deter them. This is a rational and reasonable answer. However, in reality, it may be that the person in question is afraid of the internet per se, or doesn't know how to use it, or perhaps doesn't wish to put the energy into learning what needs to be done. This account (reflecting the interests of the elephant) may in fact offer a more genuine reason for disliking online banking, even though it may refer to less noble motivations.

So, this is another example of what may be going on in the background and it is through persistent and skilled dialogue that insights can be won and the reality of the situation can be revealed. But this needs to be a routine part of business and one that importantly does not remain in the shadows of the organization. Deeper enquiries, such as those referred to earlier, need to happen in informal and formal spaces. Leaders and managers in the business may need to take a long hard look at how much of their time they devote to operating in formal spaces, because if the majority of their time is spent in meetings, at presentations, at pre-arranged events and so on then they will be missing out on a large slice of reality that the rest of the organization has to offer.

The value of discourse across multiple fora and platforms

We have talked about the value of bringing thought and information from the informal space into the formal space and bringing the 'shadowside' of an organization into plain view. However, as two separate worlds that have grown up in parallel, often shaping each other but rarely in direct communication, it can be difficult to see how to do this.

There are also strong normative restraints acting upon subject matter and delivery in traditional, formal fora that can act as barriers to high quality dialogue. For example, communication in a board meeting will usually have a bias towards presenting and reporting, rather than discussion. There will be a preponderance of factual information and little talk about feelings, and the formality and ritual can be disconcerting for more junior members of the organization who may feel the need to be deferential, or simply cannot see the benefit of such an approach.

Managers should think creatively about maximizing the opportunities for people to engage in dialogue, and introduce as many textures as possible. It is not enough to provide mere square footage for some multitasking 'meeting room' without paying attention to the kinds of conversation that may take place there.

Varying the physical context where people can talk can create a variety of tones where the line between the informal and the formal can be blurred. For example, the success of 'chill-out' areas within organizations is well documented and an increasing requirement in the creative and technology industries where they are seen as essential to the creative process and contributory factors to the responsiveness and agility that characterizes these fields.

Certain conversations may require a level of safety and privacy that these types of informal spaces can provide. An empty boardroom can exert a residual power by association and can be an inhibiting space for many. Likewise, a small meeting room normally used for appraisal disclosures, disciplinary meetings and job interviews is not a very inviting space for a brainstorming session about an exciting new product.

Creating occasions where employees can access senior staff in an informal setting, away from the symbols of deference, can lead to deeper conversation about the views, ideas and ambitions that are held by individuals for themselves and the organization.

Technology should not be avoided here and organizations that seek to limit social media access do so at their peril. Existing platforms such as Twitter can provide a stream of 'as it happens' information, as opposed to having to wait until the next scheduled meeting when a crisis or opportunity has passed. Greater Manchester Fire and Rescue Service in the United Kingdom for example, use Twitter with great innovation, as a first line media relations channel, to build and maintain the relationship with the local community and as an early warning system to alert them to an incident.

Many younger members of an organization may feel more comfortable using e-mail and text, as this is their preferred method of communication outside of the office. Those with more extraverted personalities may appreciate face-to-face time. Offering multi-channel opportunities for dialogue, not only allows the informal to be heard, but also enables employees to select the communication method that they find to be the most natural in the moment. Not only does this ability to choose remove the barrier of discomfort, for the individual, from any dialogue, but also this is an essential part of the Freedom to Actualize that we will talk about later.

The opportunity offered by everyday conversational tools and techniques

Much of the discussion so far in this chapter has referred to the Freedom to Speak as it arises through conversation and natural exchanges. This accounts for the majority of the ways in which perspectives are shared in the workplace, and beyond. But there are tools, techniques and frameworks that are designed explicitly to facilitate exploration and problem solving and these can be very useful. In order for these to work, the parties involved (usually two or more people) need to understand the techniques they plan to use, and have agreed to do so. This may seem like an obvious observation to make but very often there can be a strong reaction in meetings if people feel that a method has been imposed upon them, or if they don't understand how to get the best from it.

The value of many of the tools available is that they provide a legitimate space for particular types of ideas to be offered. For example, with Edward de Bono's Thinking Hats (below) the technique invites, at one point, the feelings and emotions people have on a topic (under the Red Hat). Devices like this can help enormously if under normal conditions it might seem counter-cultural (but nevertheless important) to speak in these terms. Also, as with Force Field Analysis (below), some frameworks remind us that results can be achieved as much by removing effort or obstacles as introducing particular interventions that push towards an outcome.

There are many tools of this sort that can add value to the quality of discussion, and we leave you with a few examples below (non-exhaustive):

- Edward de Bono's Six Thinking Hats (particularly useful for evaluating ideas/propositions and shaping a course of action).
- Kurt Lewin's Force Field Analysis (useful for mapping the forces that drive an outcome and those that restrain an outcome).
- Barry Johnson's Polarity Management framework (useful for understanding the relationship between seemingly opposing possibilities, eg high quality and low cost).
- David Cooperrider's 4-D Model (useful for developing possibilities that emphasize strengths and the ability to dream).
- Cognitive Mapping (useful for a mapping, in a fluid sense, the meaning people give to particular ideas and the interrelations between them).

Key questions to help develop your Freedom to Speak (F2S)

1 What might be the obstacles that get in the way of you sharing your views and ideas with colleagues in the organization, and how might you start to remove these?

2 What might be the obstacles that get in the way of you engaging in deeper conversations about the organization and your role in it, and how might you start to remove these?

3 Do you feel that you know enough about the meaning and the value of the work you do? How can you find out more and then act on this information?

4 Which Intended Domains of Value Creation (IDVC) could you add even greater value to?

5 What steps might you take to reduce the level of deference in the organization? Which elements of the SPEED model in particular would you want to prioritize?

6 What can you do to ensure that conversation is conducted on an adult-to-adult basis (direct, on the same level, transparent, reasoned) rather than on a parent–child basis?

7 How can you broaden your repertoire of thinking and conversational styles and minimize your use of styles such as 'deficit thinking'?

8 How can you regulate the appropriate use of technical and corporate language?

9 How might you engage more often in deeper, more reflective conversations about what is happening in the background of the organization, ie what is *really* going on, and importantly ensure that this reality is discussed in the formal spaces of the organization?

10 How might you vary the 'texture' of discussions by paying attention to the different fora and platforms available, eg 'chillout' spaces, webrooms etc.

11 Might the use of different problem solving and conversational tools, eg Edward de Bono's Six Hats, help in raising the quality of some of your discussions?

Notes

1 Orwell, G (1949/2003) *Nineteen Eighty-Four*, Penguin Books, p 60.

2 Ryde, R (2012) *Never Mind the Bosses: Hastening the death of deference for business success*, Wiley & Sons.

3 www.telegraph.co.uk/finance/newsbysector/banksandfinance/9368430/Libor-scandal-How-I-manipulated-the-bank-borrowing-rate.html

4 www.fsa.gov.uk/static/pubs/final/barclays-jun12.pdf

The third freedom
The Freedom to Actualize

06

I want you to picture the scene of the day that you retire from your last job. It is the day when you will deliver a retirement speech. All of your colleagues will be gathered around to hear how you reflect on the people you've worked with, what you will miss most and what sense you've made out of the hours, days, weeks, months and years you've put into the job. Many will be curious to know what it must feel like to be able to get off the hamster wheel of work and live a different life. Others will wonder what you will do next. Some may picture themselves, in the same place where you are standing now, and they will wonder whether they will reach the same conclusions about the experience of working as you. We started this chapter by saying that 'most people spend most of their waking hours in work'. And this is the very moment when you break the cycle. As you imagine yourself on your retirement day looking back at your career, ask yourself these questions:

1 How do I feel?

2 What am I most proud of?

3 What did I accomplish?

4 What might be my legacy?

5 How did work change me?

6 Did people get to know the *real* me?

7 Do I know the *real* me?

8 Do I feel ready to move on?

9 Did I act authentically?

10 Am I happy with myself about what I did at work, and how I did it?

The Freedom to Actualize (F2A) identified as the third element to the Freedoms Model was explained earlier as: 'The freedom to assume and realize an identity and perspective that is different from others' and reflects your own emergent personality and values.'

This is true. But as the list of retirement day questions suggests, it is more than this. When we think of the Freedom to Actualize it is helpful to picture this as having four aspects (Figure 6.1), with associated freedoms:

- *To be.* This refers to the extent to which people are able to assume and express their identity and personality at work. This may be manifest in a number of ways ranging from how people dress to the way that individual skills are brought into work.

- *To discover.* This refers to the opportunity that work allows for people to gain an appreciation of their unique preferences, skills and interests, as well as to discover at a deeper level the meaning of what they do.

- *To imagine.* This refers to the extent to which works provides a space and the encouragement for people to develop possibilities, explore ideas and to imagine how they might develop and grow.

- *To become.* This refers to the encouragement, acceptance and facilitation that work offers for people to re-shape their identities and practically realize their potential as individuals (to be applied more broadly than the workplace alone).

FIGURE 6.1 A representation of the different aspects of the Freedom to Actualize

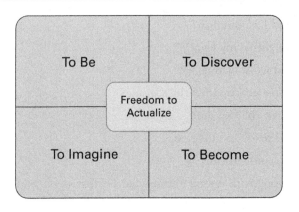

We recognize that it is at this point in the chapter where some readers may find this particular definition of the Freedom to Actualize as something they associate with a more west coast, Californian, and bohemian preoccupation. And it is unfortunate in some senses if this is where interest ends because the artificial division between the work self and the non-work self is exactly the problem that the Freedom to Actualize is seeking to solve. The schism discussed at the outset to this book is real and it is born from the idea that the set of experiences, aspirations and feelings that relate to our non-work self have little to do with the experiences, aspirations and feelings that we associate with our work self. In this way, to divide them and keep them separate is seen as a logical step to take. But this, of course, doesn't stand up to analysis. The only difference between the two worlds is the purpose to which the same body of experiences, aspirations and feelings[1] are put. And once we recognize this merger between the two worlds, and also hold in our heads the fact that most people spend most of their waking hours in work, then the case for exploring the person you are, and the person you become in work, is very powerful.

Benefits of the Freedom to Actualize

The benefits of exercising the Freedom to Actualize are felt at the individual level, at the level of organizational culture, and more broadly at the organization level (with regard to its mission, prosperity etc). Of the three Freedoms the Freedom to Actualize can create the most profound impact on organizational life and we might think, in particular, of the following clusters of benefits arising. As you read these consider how you would feel in an environment of high actualization and what benefits might arise for you:

- Well-being, happiness and engagement: organizations where people do not feel alienated from their work, where they do not feel psychological dissonance (between work and their true selves), and where they can become fulfilled through learning and growth, generate a greater sense of well-being and happiness. In turn these benefits have a positive effect on absenteeism, presenteeism and engagement. The well-being literature (for example, offered by Professor Martin Seligman), and the detailed research into employee engagement, is absolutely clear on the positive relationship between these variables.

- Connectedness to the external environment: with a workforce that continually seeks growth and deeper understanding, and one that is minded to draw a variety of external interests and passions into the organization, we see much greater connectedness to the twists and turns of the operating environment. And in an environment that we described earlier as permanently 'slushy' (as contrasted with Kurt Lewin's freeze-unfreeze-re-freeze model) organizations need employees that have their hands on technological, cultural, generational etc shifts outside the walls of the business. This is one reason why, for example, there is wisdom in the principle of Google Time (20 per cent special projects time allowance) which forces a relationship with events and interests that don't appear on the daily task sheet of employees.

- A broad set of constantly evolving capabilities: in an environment where learning in its broadest sense is prized, and where people are actively engaged in understanding and sharpening their own talents, the result is an organization with a broad and deep set of capabilities. These are capabilities that can be added to the functional and necessary skills involved in getting the job done.

- Self-awareness and mindfulness: as individuals exercise their Freedom to Actualize it follows that they will gain greater awareness of themselves and how they impact on others. Most organizations these days have accepted the importance of Emotional Intelligence, for example, to their success. Emotional Intelligence depends on people building their skills in self-awareness, interpersonal awareness, self-management and relationship management. In fact most modern organizations have systematized this broader ambition through processes such as 360 degree feedback, the use of psychometrics (such as Myers-Briggs Type Indicator), executive coaching and so on. These are important qualities that have a direct impact on, for example, our effectiveness in dealing with clients and customers, as well as how we handle relations with colleagues.

- Diversity: an inevitable and strongly desirable consequence of exercising the Freedom to Actualize is the diversity of styles, qualities, interests and passions that will arise. Diversity is a highly valuable asset for an organization to possess. We see levels of innovation and creativity being positively affected by diversity. We see the prospect of greater representatives of the clients and customers we serve arising through diversity. We see the prospect of a richer debate and a higher quality of dialogue. We see the risks of Group Think being mitigated.

- Talent attraction and retention: in the research for this book there was no shortage of support for the idea that people are more likely to join and stay with organizations that allow them to be authentic – to be themselves. And the converse is true also, in that people who feel that their personality is being squeezed or distorted by the experience of work are more likely to leave. We are also seeing a rise in the priority that people give to the opportunities that organizations offer to learn and grow (personally and professionally). Research into the aspirations and motivations of Generation Y job-searchers, for example undertaken by the recruitment giant Adecco,[2] have highlighted repeatedly that learning and growth are a priority area (68 per cent cited growth and development) and a key differentiator between prospective employers.

- Moral obligation: this is a consideration that could appear at either the bottom or the top of a list of reasons for pursuing the Freedom to Actualize. Our view is that the moral dimension is a fundamental motivation for wanting to get this right. Work is a moral issue for a number of reasons. First, people give over an enormous amount of themselves to work, eg their time, energy, emotions, ideas etc (in many cases most of their available energy, time etc). Secondly, for many, work is how people define their self-worth. This is a point illustrated very well in circumstances when people find themselves unemployed. Thirdly, the product of our labour shapes the world as it is today – from the medical care we give to people that are unwell, to the food we eat, and to the cars we drive in. Much of what you see around you has come to be through human labour and ingenuity (for example, in creating machinery to make products). Work is political also. Workers enter into an employment agreement that generates a particular distribution of power (usually in favour of the employer), and employees are required to accept conditions that shape where they should work, when they should work, how they can make decisions, how they should behave, what processes they should follow and so on. And of course the political dimension runs much deeper than this (more on this later). Our view therefore is that employers and employees should support and exercise the Freedom to Actualize for both the practical and moral reasons explored.

A final observation to make about these benefits is who else would you want to see exercising the Freedom to Operate (F2O) and the Freedom to Speak (F2S) if not people who have actively learned, developed, understood themselves, sought out the meaning in their work, were open to change and were connected to the outside world?

Let us look in a little more detail at each of the four quadrants of the Freedom to Actualize concept.

Considering ways 'to be': Self-expression

Unlike the previous freedoms, that is the Freedom to Operate (F2O) and the Freedom to Speak (F2S), the Freedom to Actualize (F2A) invites some deeper philosophical and psychological questions. We can treat the process of Actualization as working on a number of levels. For example, for many people it will be a matter of great importance that they are able to dress as they choose in work – as a way to express themselves. From one perspective this might be judged to be a rather superficial aspiration, but at another level we can see, and can treat this as a manifestation of a particular set of values: a sense of identity, of belonging, of meaningful personal experiences, and so on. And we know this to be true by looking in semiotic terms to the symbols and signifiers found in clothing more generally. The clothes worn by the Cabin Crew of airlines such as Virgin, for example, signify youthfulness, cool, glamour, individuality (a 'splash of red in a sea of grey') and so on. The military, for example, use clothing to symbolize a range of values and beliefs such as the importance of authority, uniformity, allegiance, order, strength, honour and so on. The external appearance of people tells us a lot about what is, or is suggested is, going on inside, and individuals will have differing orientations in wanting to articulate their inner self in the workplace.

But this is not clearly just about clothing. Equally, we might exchange the way we dress as an important form of self-expression for using the words and expressions that feel most natural to us, or engaging with customers in a way that reflects our personality, or the manner in which we consult with others on projects. At a deeper level still, the form that our self-expression takes might be about the political views we hold, our perspectives on what matters most in our work, our sexuality, religious beliefs or the life experiences that have made us what we are. The question though that is central to all of these dimensions of self-expression is to what extent we are able to exercise this freedom; what are the boundaries of possibility?

In relation to the Freedom to Operate earlier we discussed the notion of the Absolute and the Residual Freedom to Operate, which involves a process of creatively challenging both, as they relate respectively to the organization, and to the role we fulfil. This is our first port of call in reflecting on the intention 'to be' ourselves at work. In the context of the example of dress as an expression of ourselves (values, identity, personality, belonging etc) we encourage the same level of enquiry and challenge to the prevailing expectations about dress. Two examples from research interviews help to illustrate the point:

> It is funny really when I look back at my assumptions about how I had to dress. I used to think that I had to wear a suit and tie. It's strange really, I thought if I want to look credible and like a serious person then I had to wear a suit, with black shoes, a tie and all the stuff that goes with it – like a briefcase and umbrella and so on. For some reason I thought this was what you do. But it always felt weird for me. I felt stiff and awkward and like I was someone else. Some time later, sadly a few years, I plucked up the courage first to dress without a tie, and then I wore smartish jeans instead of suit trousers, and dumped the briefcase for a more casual bag. And not only did I feel much more like me, but nothing bad happened. No one thought I was an idiot or an impostor. No one looked at me in an odd way, they just accepted it. Why it took me so long I don't know but I'm really pleased I did this. It sounds like a small thing, but it wasn't to me. (A junior auditor)

> We sometimes think we need to be different people to be more acceptable to others. This is usually bullshit though, and almost always ends up being an unpleasant experience. We're more successful, and happier when we are [being ourselves] and less fulfilled when we make compromises because we think we should. (Creative Director)

The Freedom to Actualize is about enabling and inviting people to be themselves as much as they would like to in the workplace; and by doing this people are closer to becoming authentic. At the same time, and as with each of the three Freedoms, there are obligations that belong to those exercising freedom.

For example, the obligation of personal accountability requires that we understand and take responsibility for the impact of the actions that we might take. This situates us in an adult-to-adult relationship with those around us. Similarly, we may wish to pay attention to the obligation related to risk and to consider the risks (to others, to the business, to ourselves) that we entertain, and the steps we might take to de-risk our actions. One approach to de-risking for example might involve making incremental, rather than big step, changes. The more that we act upon the Freedom to

Actualize the more that the Freedom to Speak comes into view too. The quality of dialogue that we have is important in this context, and furthermore is a critical sense making mechanism that needs to be activated as people bring greater levels of authenticity to the workplace.

Much of what we know about the workplace is that in formalizing processes, titles, behaviours, objectives etc workers can find themselves increasingly distanced from their work and from other people. The word 'role' is interesting in this regard. The verbs that usually precede the word 'role' tell us a lot about it – typically we can:

- play 'a role';
- act 'a role';
- assume 'a role';
- adopt 'a role'; and
- portray 'a role' etc.

There are some interesting implications of these words. Firstly, the actor and the act are deliberately separated from one another. Secondly, the language of acting, playing and portraying suggest that the actor may not, and in fact most likely does not, mean what they are saying; they are either following a script that they have not authored, or they are adopting a demeanour that is not fully theirs. In the sea of authenticity therefore we immediately encounter some rocks.

Broadening out from the notion of role to the experience of work, we see other variables that seek to drive a wedge between who we are, what we do and the way we do it. For example, our position in the hierarchy places expectations upon us. The seemingly limitless set of organizational processes we have to engage with, dictate how we spend much of our time. The communication conventions found in the organization, from formal minutes, reports and e-mail protocols to proposal documents, performance appraisal meetings and agendas put us in a pre-constructed relationship to one another. The total experience of work is one that involves turning otherwise natural, free flowing, unbounded and emergent interactions into structured, organized, demarcated and managed interactions. Much of this is clearly for very good reason. But one consequence arising from this of particular importance is what Walt Whitman would describe as: '[A resulting] cold and bloodless intellectuality.'[3]

Organizations very often create machines out of people. The relentless search for productivity, efficiency and deliverables, combined with the strictures of processes, hierarchy, roles and all other organizing mechanisms, has a de-humanizing effect. Whether working in service or commodity industries, workers are resources in a production process that are obliged to submit to artificial and externally imposed routines. Workers play roles, they comply with rules, and they hand away the product of their labour. Colleagues will engage with one another in the meeting room in a controlled, unemotional and dispassionate manner, but outside the meeting, outside of the formal organization, are free to be natural, emotional and real, or for that matter, to choose whatever mode they wish to.

The experience of work is one that can be alienating. Workers become outsiders in their own lives and, as Karl Marx would argue, this represents a 'loss of reality' to the worker:

> The object that labour produces, its product, stands opposed to it as something alien, as a power independent of the producer. The product of labour is labour embodied and made material in the object, it is the objectification of labour. The realisation of labour is its objectification. In the sphere of political economy this realisation of labour appears as a loss of reality for the worker, objectification as a loss of and bondage to the object, and appropriation as estrangement, as alienation.[4] (Marx, 1844)

With the call to actualize, we encourage employees 'to be' through a process of self-expression, one that will see values, an identity, beliefs and personality becoming manifest in a variety of ways, from the clothes that are worn to the ideas that an individual will articulate. Furthermore, and borrowing the principles of the Absolute and Residual Freedom to Operate, we invite workers to creatively challenge assumptions about what is permissible. It is worth bearing in mind that the constraints that are thought to be 'in the way' might both be external to, or internal to, the individual. We also call upon workers to re-humanize the workplace, to replace an often 'cold and bloodless' environment with one that goes some way to restoring the 'reality' of the non-work environment. In practice this may be a gradual process and one that also invokes the obligations discussed earlier, such as the need to de-risk whatever is done. But our view is that the best way to 'get real' and to 'be real' at work is not to be complicit in going through the motions.

Considering ways 'to be': Fit and alignment

In the research undertaken for this book we encountered a number of people that 'scored' highly in the areas of the Freedom to Operate (F2O) and the Freedom to Speak (F2S), but scored less well on the Freedom to Actualize (F2A). Interestingly, this was not because they couldn't express their personalities at work, or because they hadn't looked to 'de-mechanize' their work experience. Rather, it was because they suspected, at a deeper level, that their values, or their self-identity, were not in tune with the organization. In more extreme cases there was a clash of values that created some serious tensions. One example illustrative of this relates to an organization where a high-profile breach of values had been discovered:

When values collide

This example is based on an experience of a high-profile organization that had, ostensibly, been successful for many years. The workforce were a well-trained and professional body of people, and similarly the senior team, along with the CEO were competent and sharply focused on the job in hand. For some years the organization had been led from the top in a thoughtful way and there had been various experiments and strategies to build the capabilities of the workforce, to share power more widely and to make a valuable contribution to stakeholders. A lot of senior management time had been spent on building the strength and capacity of the organization.

The employees of the organization were value-driven and cared deeply about delivering meaningful results in what they did. Although like most organizations, the organization had its quota of single-word, weighty values (openness, honesty, trust etc) laminated and pinned to the walls, in this particular organization these values were meant. They were not simply messages crafted to the outside world to gain support or backing, rather they were values that were genuinely owned and honoured by the workforce. There was a good level of pride in the organization. Things, it was felt, could certainly improve, but the organization functioned well.

Up until this point most employees would have said that their personal values matched, by and large, the espoused and lived values of the organization. There was a good fit and alignment. That was until one morning the workforce found out about a serious breach in the values of the organization. The news came to them first as they read the front page of a local newspaper, and much to the surprise of everyone in the organization, the newspapers reported that a member of staff had been involved in downloading and sharing illegal and sexually explicit materials using laptops owned by the organization, and during working hours. To make this worse the material was of a particularly unpleasant nature and as the story unfolded the allegations got worse. The biggest news of all though was that the claims were addressed to the CEO who, it was alleged, had been personally responsible for all of the activities reported.

In a relatively short amount of time the CEO was temporarily suspended, then dismissed and the case became a criminal prosecution. Some six months later the CEO was sentenced to prison for just under a year, and a new, external CEO was shipped in to take over. This then led to a host of other accusations and measures taken to look at how this kind of activity was concealed, who else was involved and how the breaches were allowed to happen.

The significance of the story in the context of authenticity, and the values held by staff in the organization, was the effect that then took hold. Very many people in the organization found it difficult to square their personal values, those that were espoused by the organization and the conduct of the CEO who, in many ways, was the most visible manifestation of the organization. In various formal and informal surveys that followed, it was clear that levels of trust in senior management had declined rapidly, the level of pride in the organization had fallen, and workers felt compromised, often feeling unable to even openly identify which organization they worked for when engaging in conversations with acquaintances outside of the organization. In this situation, the values that people stood for could not have been more seriously shattered, and along with this came a conundrum for many people. Employees could clearly articulate their concerns. How can we continue to work in an organization where this kind of thing can happen? What else might have been going on, and what other values might have been abused in the process? What is the point in having values if they are not observed?

In this kind of situation the Freedom to Actualize, and the elements associated with it, eg self-expression, may simply not be enough on their own for people. And so in this instance, for some, it may be that the most appropriate way to exercise the Freedom to Actualize is to leave the organization and find an employer where there is a closer match between espoused and lived organizational values and those of the individual. For others however, this may not represent a sufficiently problematic breach of values, or misalignment with personal values, to motivate them to leave the organization. In fact, it may serve to mobilize effort to ensure that breaches of this nature are not allowed to occur again in the organization. But in both scenarios we witness a decision-making process that is triggered by a breach of values.

The values that organizations articulate are typically generic in nature and most organizations make claim to similar kinds of values, eg integrity, innovation, customer-service etc. However, the personal values that people hold tend to be more diverse, more specific and, well, more personal. For example, whereas some people believe deeply in fairness and justice, others might prioritize creativity, whereas some people are motivated by service to others, a strong work ethic might be an abiding value for others. Some of the research contributions for this book implicitly highlight tensions between values at the personal and the organizational level:

> I am not particularly fulfilled in my job and when I think about this it might not be the company per se that I am unhappy with, but the industry. (Editor, Medical Publications)

> My organization likes to believe that it is better at providing and encouraging [the freedom to be authentic] than it actually is. [Staff in the organisation] work on fear, fear of getting something wrong, fear of saying something they shouldn't, fear of losing their job... I will leave if I manage to muster the confidence to do so. (Banking Division)

> My organization's core values are Collaboration, Outcomes, Respect and Engagement; all sentiments I agree with. Unfortunately, I don't think my organization is doing a good job of following those values right now. My own personal tenet, which is treat others as you want them to treat you, doesn't seem to exist within the way people work in the Department. I have seen some terrible behaviour that has no negative consequence. It just amazes me. (Specialist adviser in large organization)

These kinds of perspectives were not uncommon in the research group for this work. Borrowing elements of the Libertarian and the Existentialist position discussed earlier we feel that where a meaningful misalignment exists between personal values or self-identity and organizational values, then action must follow. And action may come in one of three forms; either we make a change (perhaps in the way we think) in order to accommodate the values of the organization, we take action to change the values of the organization, or we make the decision and act to leave the organization, ie we either accept it, change it or leave. While this seems quite confronting as a set of choices, for many that we have spoken to, this framing of the implications can be very empowering.

Considering ways 'to be': Keeping in flow

The concept of 'flow' was developed by Mihaly Csikszentmihalyi, a psychology professor at the University of Chicago, who proposed that optimal performance in all of us occurs at a time when we are fully immersed in an activity to the point that we achieve a sense of oneness with that activity. In such a mental state, time flies by, there is a falling away of ego, there are deep levels of concentration and there is a great sense of accomplishment.

In a non-work setting we might think of the activity of scuba diving giving rise to a flow experience; we can think of the need for moment-to-moment alertness of the body as it moves in the water, the minute shifts in current, the slow, deliberate act of breathing in and out and the crackle of air bubbles as they pop near the divers' ears, the changes to air supply levels on the equipment dials, how divers communicate with one another with clear and pronounced hand signals, and the sense of being utterly immersed in another world. Writing a report or a book, for example, might be another example of a flow experience. The author is fully occupied by the task. Sounds outside the office or room, that might otherwise cause distraction, go completely unnoticed. Hours pass in what seems like minutes. The author is given over entirely to the experience and may not even remember to stop for lunch or take a break. Finally when the author stops their work the bright morning light of the sun has turned to the soft, purple light of dusk. These are examples of flow.

For some people experiences such as these will be rare in the workplace, and for some, they may never happen. But Csikszentmihalyi might argue that if we are in flow we are highly motivated, energized, engaged and may even encounter feelings of joy and rapture. Perhaps above all though, we are fully in the state of 'being'. It is for this reason the flow is of interest to the Freedom to Actualize and the ability 'to be' in the workplace.

However, what gives rise to flow experiences will be different for different people and in the same way that we considered fit between organizational and personal values, we can pose for ourselves the same question regarding the ability to be in flow, that is:

- Does my work enable me to be in flow?

- Is my role a good fit with me when I think about it in terms of flow?

- To the extent that I do experience flow, what am I doing when this happens?

- Are there particular elements of my role that engender a flow experience?

- Are there particular working arrangements, eg working alone/with people, in the office/at home, close/distant management oversight etc where it is easier for me to get into flow?

Considering ways 'to be': The distorting effects of defensiveness and self-protectiveness

An important variable, not yet discussed, that relates to our ability 'to be' in the workplace is the presence, or not, of defensiveness. The reasons for feeling defensive in work are wide-ranging and we might think of this impulse to 'self-protect' as being triggered in a number of ways, such as:

- a fear of being criticized/attacked;
- a fear of being manipulated/bullied;
- a fear of unfair/unjust treatment;
- a fear of failure;
- a fear of loss, eg job, role, status etc;
- a fear of not being recognized for effort/contribution; and
- a fear that others might be unfairly treated unless you act to defend them.

In circumstances such as these, it is commonplace for a variety of coping behaviours to emerge. So for example, if a worker anticipates criticism, they may alter their behaviour and the way they choose 'to be' in a variety of ways which might include:

- second guessing what a colleague/manager wants to hear (and telling them what they want to hear);
- revealing only the palatable elements of their views to avoid disagreement;
- excessive evidence gathering to substantiate their position;
- recruiting the support or views of others to give their views weight;
- imagining criticisms and slights that aren't there; and
- quickly becoming argumentative.

In the context of the Freedom to Actualize and the ability 'to be' at work, we treat these as 'distorting behaviours' as they serve to mask, misrepresent, sublimate or otherwise change the behaviours that would naturally, and more authentically, occur. Furthermore, they commit us to a path of game playing in the workplace by which we mean that workers assume a position that may not reflect their true perspective because they anticipate the negative consequences of the fear they hold. The more that this happens, and the more that people enter into game playing, the less able they are to be authentic. Over time, it is perhaps no surprise that workers can become estranged from the workplace and 'bent out of shape'.

The solution to this lies both with the individual and with management. It is in the interests of both groups to minimize the motivation towards defensiveness and self-protection. Earlier we discussed 'defensive routines' in the context of how we speak with one another. Specifically, we explored the potentially damaging effect of 'deficit thinking', and so if we are looking to reduce defensiveness, there is a strong argument for replacing deficit thinking with a broader repertoire of thinking/engagement styles. The same would apply to the inappropriate use of corporate and technical jargon, which too can generate defensive behaviour. Other irritants in the organizational system include competitive behaviour, micro-management, heavy process requirements and perhaps unsurprisingly, where there is limited Freedom to Operate and limited Freedom to Speak.

Considering ways 'to discover and to imagine': Raising self-awareness

Starting from the position that work occupies most of our waking hours, it is perhaps no surprise that work becomes a critical place of learning and growth. And this may arise because of work, or in some circumstances despite work. What can be learned is almost without limit, and we can think of a combination of factors creating this web of possibilities including:

- type of organization (and what it is seeking to accomplish);
- type of role;
- our individual determination to learn and grow;
- our enacted Freedom to Operate; and
- the support and backing of management/the organization etc.

Here are some examples of how people have reflected on the way that work has changed them:

[Because of work] I'm much more diplomatic than I used to be and take a lot of time to understand the world view and values of the people I am working with, so my listening skills are pretty good. I am very curious about what motivates, excites and troubles people. I am far less judgmental and much more compassionate than I used to be, and am a lot less fearful than I used to be. (Leadership Trainer)

[In some ways] working in the organization has changed me negatively, because I feel I have actually relaxed the usually high standards of performance I set for myself. I've learnt a lot about process and how to communicate and negotiate with people who are not part of my own 'tribe'. [However] In my career over the past 25 years, I have learnt how to remain self-motivated, to focus on constant professional development and learning, and to remain humble. Medicine teaches you very early in life that bad things can happen to good people and so I learnt to be grateful for what I have, not to take good fortune for granted, and to always be respectful. (Medical Adviser)

It has made me more determined, and possibly also more aware of the inequalities in society... You have to learn to be bullish and be ready to encounter people who have a sense of entitlement that might not be based on talent. (PR Account Director)

Essential though to all of this is the way in which work offers an environment and a set of provocations that raise our self-awareness. All of these quotes point to a process of self-discovery that work has mediated in some way. Work provides us with a number of lenses to view the world, whether they are focused on the particular clients that the organization serves or the behaviours of colleagues, and we find ourselves observing people and events and then reflecting on our own relationship to them.

Modern organizations that have made use of processes such as 360 degree feedback, psychometrics, executive coaching, team-building training and so on have understood the importance of self-awareness. The investment in concepts such as Daniel Goleman's Emotional Intelligence underscores this attention to self-awareness. At a more formal level the habit of performance appraisal and management is intended to facilitate greater self-understanding and a commitment to learning and growth.

Our framing though of the Freedom to Actualize and the ambition 'to discover' and 'to imagine' both includes and goes beyond these strategies for raising self-awareness. Most of these approaches are in place in order to shape behaviours in ways that might lead to more effective relationships internally and externally to the organization. This is important and has a continuingly valuable contribution to make as workers build self-awareness, try out new behaviours in the process, then get feedback that tells them more about themselves, eg what they are capable of. In addition though, it is our view that individuals should reflect more deeply on the questions suggested earlier, along with others, such as:

- Discover: What is important to me about how I express myself? Eg clothes, language etc.

- Imagine: If I was able to express myself more fully, what would I be doing?

- Discover: What are my personal values, and which matter most here?

- Imagine: If my personal values were fully in place in my role, what would be different?

- Discover: What are the circumstances when I am in flow?

- Imagine: What are the smallest changes I could make to be in FLOW for much more of the time?

- Discover: What makes me happy (at work/outside of work)?

- Imagine: What habits might I develop to be happier?

Considering ways 'to be': Finding and constructing meaning

Related to the challenge of raising self-awareness, is a deeper exploration of the meaning of the work that people do. In our experience, very few people take the view that work is solely a means to an end – that being to earn money. Money, for most, is the primary reason why people go to work, but not the only reason. Other motivators include looking for social engagement, intellectual challenge, service to others and so on.

Meaning can manifest itself in a multitude of ways. One way in which this is found is when people articulate what they are proud of in work. These examples draw out the diversity of the meaning that is found:

> [I feel proud] that we have nurtured astounding outsider art... proud that we have conducted ourselves honestly and ethically... that we didn't play the game by the rules... that we tried to do no evil (no, really) and to harm no one... What matters most is the happiness and satisfaction of those involved. (A&R Person)

> [I feel proud] that we're doing a reasonable job of only working with clients that make the world a better place... [and I value] being intellectually stimulated... We're more successful, and happier when we are [authentic]... and less fulfilled when we make compromises because we think we should. (Creative Director)

I enjoy feeling that my work is valued and I like seeing the work I've produced in use by others... [and] I also like seeing how committed these people [those I help] are to their jobs and making a positive contribution to society. (Executive Education Support)

The most fulfilling issue for me is still the idea that I have the ability to influence policy relevant to all children and young people [in the region]. That is a huge privilege for me. (Medical Adviser)

I get a huge amount of satisfaction when people give positive feedback on what I make and sell. What matters is that I stay true to the original ethos of my company, which is to keep things simple. (Owner, Food Producer)

Understanding this meaning, both for the individual and for the corporate body, is supremely important.

At the individual level, we can think of there being two different sorts of meaning, namely intrinsic meaning and extrinsic meaning. Figure 6.2 develops this idea.

An activity can be thought to possess intrinsic meaning when the value that is conceived of and experienced resides within the individual. For

FIGURE 6.2 Two different types of meaning/meaning requirement at work

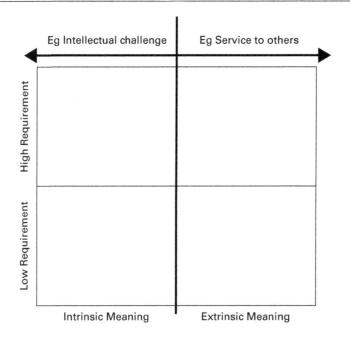

example, if a task were found to be meaningful because it is intellectually challenging then this would qualify as intrinsic meaning. If instead an individual discovered meaning in their work through the value it delivers to people or things outside of themselves then this would suggest extrinsic meaning. An example of this might be where a wedding planner finds meaning through giving people a sense of occasion and happiness.

Additionally though, Figure 6.2 invites us to consider our own personal level of requirement for intrinsic or extrinsic meaning as this will vary. Some people, for example, may care a great deal about their work providing them with a means of connecting to others and this will be significant and will represent value to them (high intrinsic meaning). Other people might care little about whether their work brings them into contact with others or, for example, that they can be creative, but will value highly their ability to make the lives of others better (high extrinsic meaning). Typically, people will score highly in at least one of the two types of meaning, and often high in both.

The argument we wish to make here is that in order to understand where we lie on the extrinsic–intrinsic axis, what our requirement is, or for that matter what we might imagine could be done to deepen our appreciation of the meaning of the work we do, we need to commit to a path of discovery and imagination ('to discover' and 'to imagine'). The encouragement that we make to individuals and managers is to undertake this work and to foster the conditions that will keep it going. As discussed earlier, the more we exercise our Freedom to Operate (F2O) and our Freedom to Speak (F2S) the more we are helped in our pursuit of meaning.

At the corporate level, meaning and purpose matters enormously. The familiar corporate mantra of mission, vision and objectives provides an insight into the importance of meaning. Unfortunately, such statements can become dry and disengaging and, in some sense, don't finish the job. This is because they fail to mine or properly develop the fullness of the concepts associated with this such as the value that is delivered (through the work of the organization), the moral and emotional implications of the organization's work, why the organizational purpose matters (beyond securing its own survival), how workers might see their place in the organization's purpose. Furthermore, there are tensions that underpin all of these dimensions of meaning such as the tension between delivering shareholder value and value to customers. The leadership of many organizations struggle with balancing this, and if they do then the rest of the organization will also. At the conclusion to this chapter we offer a short case study of an innovative UK-based advertising agency, Karmarama, who go to some lengths to articulate what they stand for.

Similarly in the field of public service there are tensions between different forms of public value. Professor Mark Moore of Harvard's Kennedy School develops thinking around this topic by using the case of a dilemma faced by a public manager. The scenario refers to a librarian working in a public library in a poorer suburb of a US city. They are carrying out their duties as a custodian of the books and learning materials in their library. One day they begin to notice certain patterns in the activities of visitors to the library. One such pattern involves the arrival of young 'latchkey' children round about late afternoon when the school day finishes. They arrive, hang around for a while, perhaps remove a few books from the shelves to give the impression of using the library for its formal purpose and then, when their parents finish work, they are picked up and taken home. The library in this example temporarily becomes a valuable childcare resource. This story is reminiscent of another similar dilemma in a public library, this time in a British town. The librarian would encounter a similar pattern but in this example with older homeless people, who, as the weather got colder, would enter the library, grab the requisite book or two to show willing, and then take off their socks and dry them on the radiators. You can imagine the scene perhaps almost too vividly. Once again, when the library had served its purpose and they were warmed up and dried out they would be able to face the cold weather again. The library in this instance was offering temporary shelter for vulnerable people. The dilemma of course is one about public value and leads us to ask the question, 'What should the librarian do?' Imagine if you were the librarian; what would you do? How would you reach a decision about the best course of action, whether this was to eject the latchkey children or the older homeless people on the grounds that they weren't using the library for its intended purpose, or do something different?

The important point is that deciding upon the value that organizations deliver, and their employees acting in different roles deliver, takes some exploration and imaginative thought. The product of this thought might be to take a different course of action or to continue on the same track, but the thinking needs to happen in the first instance. The conditions 'to discover' and 'to imagine' play a key role in this manifestation of the Freedom to Actualize.

Considering ways 'to become': Moving to action

The process underpinning the ambition 'to become' starts with movement. This is a movement that begins with discovery and imagination and takes us towards action. But there is a lot that conspires to keep us doing what we've always done, to keep us in the same position and, in a sense, to keep us in a state of somnolence. The forces that keep us in this state are many and include habit (which offers up a lot to efficiency and to predictability, but does little to inspire movement), organizational processes (which by definition, ask that we comply with what is required rather than develop different thinking), cultural norms (which tacitly introduce boundaries and conventions that corral our thinking and behaviour in the same direction), an underlying risk aversion in organizations (when it comes to facing deeper questions about meaning, personal expression etc), a limited degree of Freedom to Operate, rigid management backing etc. And these are not exhaustive.

So there is an inevitably difficult movement to make in becoming different at work. Let's be clear that this is essentially the proposal implied by the aspiration 'to become', that is, as people discover more about themselves (and at a deeper level), and as they imagine other ways in which they should develop and grow, then this will enable them to change, and to become different. 'Becoming' in this way might take many forms, such as:

- changing how we dress at work;
- talking more openly about parts of our personality or interests that were previously kept out of view;
- building or introducing new skills to be applied to the role;
- contesting corporate decisions where previously we might have remained quiet;
- managing our time differently in line with a different framing of the meaning and value of our work;
- changing the amount of attention we give to internal and external stakeholders; and
- changing our philosophical position or mindset, for example in terms of how we might manage people.

In moving to action there are three dynamics at play, although the third of these is by far the most important:

1 The first relates to an *emotional commitment* on the part of the individual to *be* different. This is described as an emotional commitment because it will involve a level of courage and a degree of personal risk that is necessarily ventured.

2 The second relates to what we call a *divergent commitment* that involves a determination to step away from the prevailing norms/processes/habits (all of which conspire to keep you there).

3 The third relates to a *practical commitment* that simply means making a real and practical change (without over-analysing, waiting for the perfect conditions or otherwise prevaricating). Our advice is wherever possible to move straight to a practical commitment (arising from the discovery and imagination processes discussed earlier). The reason for this is that there is no better way of learning from a new way of being than to try it out. Furthermore, because of the weight of existing habits and attitudes that keep us in check, the alternative very often will lead to no action at all.

Considering ways 'to become': A dynamic process

Following on from the work involved with moving to action, there needs to be an accompanying realization that the process of becoming is dynamic and never concluded. Implicit within this is the recognition that not only might a successful change in an individual be followed by another change at some point, but also the acknowledgement that not all changes will be successful. This lies at the heart of all growth and the words of Samuel Smiles (also credited to Albert Einstein) underscore this point well: 'He who never made a mistake, never made a discovery.'

The message contained in this is directed towards individuals and managers as both hold the power to make a meaningful difference, whether this is in the form of replacing criticism with learning, or through taking thoughtful steps to de-risk changes.

Considering ways 'to become': Transcending the ego

A final observation about the process of actualization relates to the focus of attention that we lend this process. Abraham Maslow developed an important psychological model based on a hierarchy of needs. At the base of this hierarchy are a fundamental set of human requirements such as food, water and sleep, with a movement upwards through needs such as security, friendship and self-esteem to the pinnacle of the triangle representing self-actualization. Over time Maslow reflected on whether self-actualization was exclusively about meeting the needs of the individual, or whether there was something that looked beyond the ego, and beyond the self. As he did this Maslow sought to clarify that self-actualization should not be confused with abandon, sensuality, hedonism and self-seeking. He emphasizes this point:

> My impression is that impulsivity, the unrestrained expression of any whim, the direct seeking for 'kicks' and for non-social and purely private pleasures ... is often mislabeled self-actualization. (Maslow, 1966)[5]

This distinction between self-seeking behaviours and aspirations that go beyond the self were expanded further by Maslow who argued that in a state of self-actualization the nature of reality could be seen more clearly and its 'essence penetrated more profoundly'. Some of the universal values that he believed could be perceived more clearly in this state included truth, goodness, beauty, unity, aliveness, perfection, justice, order and meaningfulness.[6]

With this in mind, Maslow engaged in various adaptations to his original theory that were never entirely concluded nor seen as entirely consistent with earlier concepts. However, of importance in this context is the emergence of self-transcendence as a feature at the pinnacle of Maslow's pyramid. This put some clear blue water between the criticisms of some commentators that his theory was limited to the self, and related only to satisfying the needs of the self and the true position that he took. This ushered in notions of service to others and also a transcendence of identity. This is important of course because all of the components of Maslow's hierarchy of needs, with the exception of this, are related entirely to the needs of the individual, to what the self needs and wants. Transcendence of the ego is different in nature from all the others and sees its beneficiary as sitting outside of the actor, not within.

While the concept of actualization explored in this book (and set out in the to be, discover, imagine and become model), is different from the concept of self-actualization at the peak of Maslow's hierarchy of needs, the transcendence point is one that has a place here.

There are some deeper and important philosophical differences related to the ego, to its manifestation and the plausibility of transcending it in the first instance (something that Jean Paul Sartre would dispute on the basis that the ego does not in fact reside within the individual). Notwithstanding these discussions, we see great value in incorporating within the 'to become' state of the Freedom to Actualize, an exploration and manifestation of what it means to move beyond the self (self expression, development of personality etc) towards serving the needs of others, and to an enacting a deeper set of truths that arise from this journey.

KARMARAMA CASE STUDY: AN INTERVIEW WITH DAVE BUONAGUIDI, FOUNDER AND CHIEF CREATIVE OFFICER

Karmarama is one of the leading creative independent communications agencies in the UK. The agency was founded in 2000 and, at the time of writing, is 250 people strong and responsible for a raft of successful campaigns for companies such as Costa Coffee, the BBC, British Telecom and Honda.

The agency is known for their 'Good Works' philosophy that is articulated as a commitment to only having the client's best interests at heart and to producing work that is entirely focused on improving the client's business. This means that, despite their creative talent and innovation, there is a policy of avoiding creative awards as they can generate competing agendas between client and agency. Effectiveness awards are encouraged, and in 2011 they were selected as *Marketing Week*'s Effectiveness Agency of the Year.

Karmarama's Good Works philosophy describes a desire to move away from the excesses that they feel have characterized the advertising and communications industry as self-serving and perhaps obnoxious in many eyes. This commitment to doing the right thing extends to both the way that employees experience working at the agency, and the unique working environment that they have created in their London office.

Dave Buonaguidi is the founder, chief creative officer, and the architect of the agency's culture. His career has spanned the more maverick advertising agencies and Channel 4, a television station with a ground-breaking remit of experimentation, creativity and diversity. He has sought out workplaces that have accommodated his desire to shake the frame of conventional working practices in order to open up new vistas of possibility, something he calls his 's**t kicker' mentality. Dave spoke to us about the particular ambition at Karmarama for employees to create meaningful work and to experience his version of the Freedom to Actualize in their daily work.

His formula for workplace happiness is a simple one that draws little distinction between work and non-work life: 'I want to make sure that I am enjoying my life. I know it sounds selfish, but when I am with people I like and having fun then that is pretty much all I want out of life, and if I can get paid on top then that's pretty much it.'

Before setting up the agency, Dave had come to the belief that the advertising and communications sector had become defined by a hegemony of 'white middle-class men' who had made UK advertising self-referential and often irrelevant to those outside of the industry, sometimes using client money to further their own ambitions. They saw that as both a vulnerable business model and a recipe for some of the more toxic workplaces that they had experienced. He explained, 'People don't set up businesses as a passion project any more. They do it because they want to make money, which I think is sad... Managers often don't care. All they are interested in are the type of staff who can get them the lifestyle and the car.'

Dave had previously worked in Channel 4 as Creative Director and had experienced a workplace that was driven by a shared interest in and commitment to challenging the status quo.

> When I worked at Channel 4 there was a cultural stickiness about the place so that when you walked in you thought, f**k me, we are going to make some good TV. They've got interesting programming; they've got interesting people; they've got an interesting history; they've got a really nice canteen; they're not in the centre of town... and it was these tiny intangible things that made all the difference.

These experiences have led to the Karmarama team forming an understanding that to attract like-minded people who are eager to break away from the prevailing culture they need a narrative that communicates their values and the experience of working there and to enact their values in every part of the agency. This gives rise to their much-publicized 'No W*****s' recruitment policy, which they are swift to act upon if any employees show signs of conforming to the archetype. Dave explains, 'Acting quickly sends the message that we are different.' Their consistency of approach is carried through into the design of the office workspace. All employees are housed on the same floor within one enormous space to encourage maximum collaboration and cross-fertilization of ideas. As outlined in Chapter 1, visitors enter Karmarama via a light tunnel that indicates that one should expect the unexpected, and through to a modest reception area that is refreshingly free of awards and then into the canteen where they are pitched into the heart of the agency. Once inside, the space is zoned into relaxation areas, cubby holes, open meeting spaces, traditional groupings of desks, so that people can find the setting that best suits their working need in the moment. Great efforts have been made to reinforce the message that working at Karmarama is stimulating, inclusive and fun. The senior team look indistinguishable from their colleagues and use the work spaces provided for everyone. Large artworks punctuate the office landscape, and expressions of individual creativity and ingenuity are encouraged as part of the daily life of the office. Housed behind the main workspace are a series of table tennis tables used by agency workers and serious athletes alike. There is even a tuck shop and a micro-brewery to set the scene of home-grown fun and innovation.

We make the place stand for something. 'No W*****s' in the main office space in neon. Make people feel that there is a level playing field and one agenda. Our agenda is to improve the business of our clients. Having a very clear vision to be the most interesting communications business there is. Inviting people and letting them prove that we are in an open environment and thinking can come from anywhere... When we built the new Karmarama offices we asked, why do people make the decisions they do about where they want to work? Tiny things make all the difference... We have a high collaboration level. The client is involved with the team and everyone is involved in the creative process rather than the usual 'baton passing' routine.

It is clear that fulfilment and personal growth are important when working at Karmarama.

Good people don't often leave [Karmarama] because they can see that they are in control of their own destiny.

Open and honest (adult to adult) conversation is encouraged at the agency between all staff including those in reporting lines. The close proximity of staff, together with the requirements of collaboration, fosters an understanding of individual working styles and behaviours. Accommodations are made to allow for these differences in a dynamic process of construction that contains within it great flexibility for individuals to develop and change. In this way, individuals take a shared responsibility in shaping a culture that reflects their needs in the moment.

The agency has an interesting take on how staff can frame their working relationships in order to promote more authentic communication.

How can you create an environment that is about being friends? When your mate comes in and is f****d off you support him or her. It's a support structure. You don't think about it, you just do it. Why can't it be like that in work? Why shouldn't an employer take an interest? It's common responsibility... How can you foster a level of friendly responsibility like you would have in your personal life. In your personal life, you don't waste time with arseholes, you become selective. You find people with shared interests. I love that environment because it's about being in a community like a village. The company becomes our house and we all look after it.

Within this constantly evolving environment of experimentation, construction and adjustment lies the space for individuals to pursue their own projects, to change and grow. This is actively encouraged through a raft of initiatives that are designed to expose members of the agency to new ideas. Academy K, their Ted Talk-like innovation, is a regular injection of new perspectives and thinking supplied by visiting speakers that is open to clients and the public. The Karma Life page of their website celebrates the projects and initiatives that employees have set up alongside their work. Their Krank scheme, which is reflective of a *Dragon's Den* style approach to sparking innovation within the agency, is one way in which the immense creative talents and aspirations are supported. Real company money is put behind a range of employee-led projects and more than this Karmarama offers resources, brand, and platform and so on to get projects off the ground. There are ventures to support local community gardening schemes, stalls selling healthy alternatives to fast food, regular music podcasts, fundraising events for charities. Although these projects are all driven by individuals' pursuing their own interests, they are all seen as fitting comfortably within the Karmarama vision of doing 'Good Works'. The drive to make the workplace fun and stimulating allows these projects to flourish openly and with the full approval of the agency and in acknowledgement that the potential to experience fulfilment in life is not left at the front door of the office. Of course the benefit to the agency is a contented workforce and the innovation that is nurtured in this kind of stimulating environment.

In fact, Karmarama are so comfortable with the idea that their employees will change and evolve during their time at the agency that the idea of leaving to take on different challenges is openly addressed in the office.

> *It makes me feel good when people leave to go to another agency or to set up a new business or a new life. One of the proudest things to happen to me was when a guy left to set up a small bicycle shop. I saw him the other day in his liveried van and I felt proud that someone who had worked in a com-pany that I had created, had been able to find what he really wanted to do. Sometimes knowing what you don't want to do is better than knowing what you want to do.*

The Karmarama vision of the workplace as a locus for support, fulfilment, experimentation and personal growth is in tune with the founding ambition to conduct business with honesty, integrity and positive intent. Dave articulates this simply as: 'If you try to be nice to people they will be nice to you and if you try to do something good then it will come back to you. It's karma, like the name.'

As a way of testing their workplace model they entered *The Sunday Times'* newspaper 100 Best Small Companies to Work For competition in 2011. Perhaps unsurprisingly they comfortably made the list at number 11. We watch with close interest this blended approach to work and non-work, and what we see is a real attempt to break the schism that so often eats away at authenticity.

Key questions to help develop your Freedom to Actualize (F2A)

1 When you look at the 'to be, to discover, to imagine, and to become' model, where might you need to give most attention?

2 What matters to you most in terms of how you express yourself at work, and how can you creatively challenge assumptions about what limits your self-expression?

3 What opportunities can you take to 're-humanize' your place of work so that it feels real and reflective of the personalities that work in it?

4 How close is the fit between your personal values and the lived values of the organization? If the fit isn't good enough what action does that suggest to you?

5 How often are you in 'flow', and what would need to happen to increase this?

6 What might you do to avoid succumbing to 'the distorting behaviours' that arise from defensiveness?

7 What are the most effective ways in which you can gather data that will broaden and deepen your self-awareness?

8 To what extent do you feel that you have understood the meaning and value of the work you do? Are there other ways in which your organization could deliver greater value?

9 In terms of intrinsic meaning and extrinsic meaning, what is the strength of your requirement in each area, and is work satisfying this for you?

10 When you incorporate changes arising from the process of actualization what might be involved in making a) an emotional commitment to change, b) a divergent commitment, and c) a practical commitment?

11 Consider what might be the more transcendent features (transcending ego, transcending identity etc) of actualization? What are the higher aspirations you might have and want to express through work?

Notes

1 In this we include a broad range of other qualities such as skills, interests, thinking, values etc.

2 www.adeccousa.com/articles/Adecco-Graduation-Survey-2012. html?id=200&url=/pressroom/pressreleases/pages/forms/allitems. aspx&templateurl=/AboutUs/pressroom/Pages/Press-release.aspx

3 In reference to the work of Ralph Waldo Emerson, Walt Whitman, *Prose Works, 1892*, ed Floyd Stovall (New York: New York University, Press, 1964), 2:517.

4 Marx, K (1844/1975) *Economic and Philosophic Manuscripts*, Lawrence & Wishart, London, pp 323–34.

5 Maslow, A H (1966) Comments on Dr Frankl's paper, *Journal of Humanistic Psychology*, **6** (2), pp 107–12.

6 Maslow, A H (1967) A theory of metamotivation: the biological rooting of the value-life, *Journal of Humanistic Psychology*, **7** (2), pp 93–127.

Assessing authenticity and freedoms
A self-completion diagnostic

07

In considering authenticity and the degree to which it is exercised at work, we start with a simple definition: 'Authenticity is the degree to which one is true to one's own personality, spirit, or character, despite external pressures.'

As we have demonstrated in earlier chapters though, the meaning of authenticity can be thought of in broader terms. This simple definition implies that authenticity is a state of being, and by definition that it is something that can be attained. It suggests that people can *have* authenticity, perhaps in the same way that they can have common sense or good interpersonal skills. But if we take for example the notion in this definition that 'one is true to one's own personality' we must also entertain the thought that firstly one has to come to understand one's own personality, and secondly, that the personality is subject to change. This favours a more dynamic interpretation of authenticity, one that is closer to it being a process than a state of being. With this in mind we might include within the definition the following examples:

- a process of discovering who we are;
- a process of imagining what we might be;
- a process of divining meaning in what we do;
- a process of finding our own terms of self-expression; and
- a process of breaking out of externally imposed expectations.

Taking this further, we might conceive of authenticity as involving an expression of what we have come to understand as our true self. This suggests, in a positivist sense, that the truth is out there to be found, we just have to reveal it and express it. Alternatively, from a more constructivist position, we can also conceive of authenticity arising through a process of constructing the personality, rather than finding it. This distinction is perhaps captured respectively in the difference between being and becoming.

In the existentialist tradition, authenticity possesses an even weightier meaning, principally because it sits at the heart of the philosophy. The importance of this idea is conveyed in the following quotes:

> We are born into the 'they', into a fully scripted, well-organized on-going social structure. And we will remain absorbed in the 'they' for our whole lives unless we discover how to become more authentic. If we pay attention to our vague awareness of death, this discovery of the deepest part of our beings might empower us to wrench ourselves free of the embrace of the 'they'. We can then become whole and resolute if we harness the power of guilt and death [our 'Existential Malaise'] as the driving force behind our freely chosen life-meanings.[1] (Heidegger, 1927)

> To be true to himself in relation to this eternal vocation is the highest thing a man can practise, and, as that most profound poet [Shakespeare] has said: 'Self-love is not so vile a sin as self-neglecting.' Then there is but one fault, one offence: disloyalty to his own self or the denial of his own better self.[2] (Kierkegaard, 1983)

> Man is nothing else but what he purposes, he exists only in so far as he realizes himself, he is therefore nothing else but the sum of his actions, nothing else but what his life is.[3] (Sartre, 1956)

It is for all of these reasons (the practical and the philosophical) that we offer, in humility, this book – intended to develop thinking on the topic as it relates to work – and in this short chapter we offer a diagnostic tool to offer a point of access for the reader. Our hope is that anyone, at any level in an organization, can engage with this tool in order to continue their understanding of their authenticity and where their attention might then go. In order to fully make sense of the results it is important to read the results alongside the previous freedoms chapters. And, as we articulated at the outset, we underline the principle behind our approach to authenticity that responsibility for claiming it must ultimately rest with the individual. Authenticity is rightly a concern for all, but it is for the individual to define it for themselves, to strive to attain it (should they choose to), and importantly to resist giving way to the temptation that it is the job of management to furnish it for them. Our key position is that: My authenticity sits with me, yours with you, and it is not our belief that it is anyone's responsibility to find it or 'fix it' for someone else.

This doesn't excuse or seek to minimize the importance of management in an organization, rather it reflects our philosophical stance and our intent to break the cycle of what we often see as a standoff between workers and management. Our proposal for managers follows in the next chapter.

Recognizing authenticity at an individual level

Authenticity is expressed in a number of ways and to suggest that a single manifestation of authenticity can be pinpointed and 'recognized' is to oversimplify the concept. But it may be useful nevertheless to hold a picture in our minds of what authenticity can look like at an individual level. This can be useful too in adding depth to the diagnostic results. Our perspective on this is based on the research for the book including the range of interviews conducted for it.

Recognizing authenticity at the individual level: An archetype

Individuals differ in the way that they operate and the way they 'show up' at work. This level of diversity is important not only because it provides the space for authenticity to flourish but also because organizations need difference to make sound decisions. Tension and differences are engines of progress and with them we make better decisions. What follows therefore is not to suggest that there is only one way to be authentic or only one way to express ourselves; this will always be individual and to an extent, unique, and this is what we would hope to see in any organization.

Our work in support of this book has however highlighted some common traits of authentic people and this archetype is offered as a device to draw out some of the visible behaviours that we see displayed by authentic people. As follows:

Typically, authentic people talk naturally, easily and openly about what is important to them in their lives outside of work. It might be that they are going through a rocky divorce or they are learning how to spend more time with their kids, but being in work doesn't make them feel that they cannot, and should not, raise topics that matter to them. Authentic people implicitly communicate the relationship between their work and non-work lives.

Among authentic people we also see comfort with showing vulnerability, and a willingness to recognize that they don't have all the answers. In conversation, authentic people might explain that they are feeling the pressure of work, or they might share doubts about their own capabilities in a given task. They will typically feel able to ask for help and advice and in doing so side-step the defensive routines so often adopted in the workplace. We interpret this show of vulnerability as reflecting a deeper solidity of a person that has done the work to understand who they are.

Related to this, authentic people have a good degree of self-awareness, which we hear them vocalize and explicitly name in conversation. When reporting these self-identified qualities and shortcomings, these will typically match the views of people around them. We see authentic people holding an accurate sense of who they are and how they are seen.

In work situations we observe that authentic people seem less restricted and bound by conventions. They will look to different ways of getting the job done, and they will talk of the job as if it is a constant work-in-progress. Authentic people will be more likely to dress in a way that suits their own tastes, and in doing so may look different from their colleagues. They will speak in their own words and phrases, rather than taking from a stock of corporate terms. The phrasing and style of delivery that they adopt is recognizable as having come from them. Their working patterns may be different from others' who might, for example, more closely match a 9–5 formula. Their work-focused views will draw upon their interests, passions and capabilities that have been developed outside, as well as inside, of work.

We see that authentic people appear energized and animated by what they do. Their work life is a source of motivation and they may have made a series of job moves in order to get to this position in the first place. They may have re-shaped their role over time to ensure it is a source of inspiration to them. The sense of dread that some associate with going to work is absent or less acute for authentic people. They show passion and excitement in the jobs, often doing so in a youthful and even excitable way. It is our experience that as authentic people examine, develop and try out new ideas about themselves and their work, they make mistakes and discoveries in equal measure. It is the questioning mind of authentic people that brings life and meaning to what they do.

We see authentic people as more able to offer accounts and explanations of why their work matters and how this makes a difference. They seem motivated to share the meaning of the work they do, having invested the time to get to an understanding of it. They may fight harder on particular issues having developed, over time, a keen sense of what matters to them most.

Authentic people actively pursue learning and growth, and in their interactions with people will show curiosity by asking questions and taking discussions to a deeper level. They take an interest in others and compare their perceptions of the work with those around them. People often come away from such conversations having claimed that they have learned a lot.

Authentic people typically underplay status and hierarchy in an organization. For example, they do not rely on deference in order to gain acceptance of their ideas, or invoke speaking protocols that might otherwise quieten the voices of more junior people. They often exhibit a less reverential and playful tone when speaking about corporate priorities, although this is not indicative of a lack of seriousness about, or care for, the success of the organization (in fact usually the opposite).

Observations and interpretation of diagnostic results

In interpreting the results of the following diagnostic tool, we suggest that you take on board a number of considerations:

- Bear in mind that although results will vary according to the sample examined, typically around a quarter of respondents will have 'a lot of/ wide scope to be authentic' and around half of respondents will have 'some scope to be authentic'. A final quarter will either have 'little/limited scope to be authentic or almost no/very limited scope to be authentic'.

- If you find yourself scoring in the largest single group suggesting 'some scope to be authentic' (typically accounting for around 50 per cent of respondents) you may wish to reflect on where in this range your score appears, ie closer to little/limited scope to be authentic or closer to a lot of/wide scope to be authentic'.

- Look not only to the total/overall score, but also to individual categories, that is the Freedom to Operate, to Speak and to Actualize, and to individual question scores (high and low). This will give you insights into the specific areas where attention might be given.

- Bear in mind that while the scope for improvement will clearly lie in the low scores, it is also important to validate and to consolidate the areas where you score highly.

- Consider which specific elements have a particular impact on your ability to be authentic at work and start to work on these. These will be different for different people.

- Creatively challenge your own assumptions about the opportunity for you to widen your freedoms, and consider undertaking small experiments to do this.

- Take action to explore elements of this diagnostic with your manager(s) and if you are a manager yourself take this opportunity to have a dialogue with the people that work to you.

- Take into consideration the three key commitments discussed in Chapter 6 to assist you in making changes that you think are important. These involve making:

  1 An *emotional commitment* on the part of the individual to *be* different. This is described as an emotional commitment because it will involve a level of courage and a degree of personal risk that is necessarily ventured.

  2 A *divergent commitment* that involves a determination to step away from the prevailing norms/processes/habits (all of which conspire to keep you there).

  3 A *practical commitment* that simply means making a real and practical change (without over-analysing, waiting for the perfect conditions or otherwise prevaricating). Our advice is wherever possible to move straight to a practical commitment (arising from the discovery and imagination processes discussed earlier). The reason for this is that there is no better way of learning from a new way of being than to try it out. Furthermore, because of the weight of existing habits and attitudes that keep us in check, the alternative very often will lead to no action at all.

Authenticity and freedoms diagnostic

At work, to what extent do I feel able to...

(Circle the corresponding number on the right for each question in Table 7.1.)

TABLE 7.1 Authenticity and freedoms diagnostic

	At work, to what extent do I feel able to... (*Circle the corresponding number on the right for each question*)	Not at all				To a large extent
1	Organize my working day and manage my time as I judge appropriate to the job	0	1	2	3	4
2	Raise concerns/highlight potential risks to the organization, particularly those risks that some may not wish to hear eg 'the elephant in the room'	0	1	2	3	4
3	Discuss the opportunities and scope for me to be authentic at work (to be true to myself)	0	1	2	3	4
4	Have discretion to take everyday decisions without involving more senior members of staff (within reasonable limitations)	0	1	2	3	4
5	Talk about my feelings and how they relate to my work (including being able to show vulnerability)	0	1	2	3	4
6	Arrange my physical workspace in a way that reflects who I am and the way I like to work	0	1	2	3	4
7	Solve problems and settle disputes on my own initiative (within reasonable limitations)	0	1	2	3	4
8	Talk to people more senior to me on an adult-to-adult basis and in doing so be honest, direct and authentic	0	1	2	3	4
9	Choose my own appearance (within reasonable limitations)	0	1	2	3	4
10	Identify and exploit new opportunities when they arise	0	1	2	3	4
11	Get enough access and time to speak to the right internal people	0	1	2	3	4
12	Allow my personality, eg sense of humour, to be expressed in my work	0	1	2	3	4
13	Formulate my own working practices/modus operandi	0	1	2	3	4
14	Speak against the accepted narrative (the 'party line')	0	1	2	3	4
15	Believe that my values are in harmony with those of the organization	0	1	2	3	4
16	Vary my place of work in order to work more effectively, eg working from home, coffee shop, office, train etc	0	1	2	3	4

(*continued*)

TABLE 7.1 Authenticity and freedoms diagnostic (*continued*)

	At work, to what extent do I feel able to... (*Circle the corresponding number on the right for each question*)	Not at all				To a large extent
17	Engage colleagues, at any level, in a conversation about the deeper drivers of organizational behaviour, eg culture, ethics, colleague behaviour etc	0	1	2	3	4
18	Integrate aspects of my personal life, eg values, hobbies, family, skills etc, into my working life	0	1	2	3	4
19	Create working partnerships and collaborations at my discretion and without seeking approval from others	0	1	2	3	4
20	Use the words, expressions and speech patterns that feel most natural to me (within reasonable limitations)	0	1	2	3	4
21	Evolve, grow and realize my potential as an individual (to be applied more broadly than the workplace alone)	0	1	2	3	4
22	Make an honest mistake without fearing blame or criticism	0	1	2	3	4
23	Throw out suggestions as a basis for discussion without feeling the need for them to be fully formed ie 'spitballing'	0	1	2	3	4
24	See, hear and know the value that my contribution makes in the organization	0	1	2	3	4
25	Undertake considered experiments or trials to explore better ways to get the work done	0	1	2	3	4
26	Use the methods of communication that best suit my style eg face-to-face, email, text etc	0	1	2	3	4
27	Engage colleagues and managers in conversation about the meaning of the work I do and the value it delivers	0	1	2	3	4
28	Alter or adapt my outputs where I feel that outcomes can be delivered more effectively in different ways	0	1	2	3	4
29	Hold meaningful dialogue with colleagues at all levels without feeling 'shut out' or disempowered by the use of technical language/corporate jargon	0	1	2	3	4
30	Learn and develop in the way that best suits my style	0	1	2	3	4

Creating and interpreting your profile

TABLE 7.2 Add up all of your scores

		Insert score below
Add up all of your scores in the rows shown in Section A (shaded in dark grey)	Section A	
Add up all of your scores in the rows shown in Section B (shaded in medium grey)	Section B	
Add up all of your scores in the rows shown in Section C (white background)	Section C	
Add up all your scores from Sections A, B and C	TOTAL/ OVERALL	

TABLE 7.3 Total/overall score

Insert your score below		Explanation
	Total/Overall score between 101–120	A lot of/wide scope to be authentic at work
	Total/Overall score between 81–100	Some scope to be authentic at work
	Total/Overall score between 41–80	A little/limited scope to be authentic at work
	Total/Overall score between 0–40	Almost no/very limited scope to be authentic at work

Dimensions of authenticity

TABLE 7.4 Results of the authenticity and freedoms diagnostic

Insert your scores below	Sections	Explanation
	Section A	Questions posed in this section refer to your **'Freedom to Operate'**, specifically the freedom that you have to arrange your affairs in the way you think best to accomplish your goals/carry out your role
	Score between 0–20	**PRIORITY AREA FOR ACTION**
	Score between 21–31	**WARRANTS ATTENTION**
	Score between 32–40	**KEEP IN VIEW**
	Section B	Questions posed in this section refer to your **'Freedom to Speak'**, specifically the freedom to offer your views in a way which isn't censored or constrained by others, in particular by those at higher levels in the hierarchy
	Score between 0–20	**PRIORITY AREA FOR ACTION**
	Score between 21–31	**WARRANTS ATTENTION**
	Score between 32–40	**KEEP IN VIEW**

(continued)

TABLE 7.4 Results of the authenticity and freedoms diagnostic (*continued*)

Insert your scores below	Sections	Explanation
	Section C	Questions posed in this section refer to your **'Freedom to Actualize'**, specifically the freedom to assume and realize an identity and perspective that is different from others' and reflects your own emergent personality and values
	Score between 0–20	**PRIORITY AREA FOR ACTION**
	Score between 21–31	**WARRANTS ATTENTION**
	Score between 32–40	**KEEP IN VIEW**

Notes

1 Heidegger M (1927/1962) *Being and Time*. Macquarrie J, Robinson E, translators, HarperCollins, San Francisco.

2 *The Sickness Unto Death: A Christian psychological exposition for upbuilding and awakening* (Kierkegaard's Writings, Vol 19), Princeton University Press (1 November 1983).

3 Kaufman, W (ed) (1956/1989) *Existentialism from Dostoyevsky to Sartre*, Meridian Publishing Company.

The management task in authentic organizations

08

We can't solve problems by using the same kind of thinking we used when we created them.

ALBERT EINSTEIN

The management task that should sit alongside the pursuit of authenticity, at least in the terms presented in this book, needs to be different from what we have come to understand as the 'job of management'.

The most fundamental concern we have with the way in which management is traditionally conceived is that it works in opposition to many of the basic tenets of workplace authenticity. In very many cases, it simply blocks authenticity from happening, and for this reason alone it may need redefinition and a serious overhaul. But more generally management needs to be looked at again in the context of a very different operating environment from the one that we encountered a few decades ago. Building on Albert Einstein's observation, if we fail to correctly apprehend the current situation that we are in, and instead assume it is the same one that we faced yesterday requiring the same remedies, we are unlikely to be successful. One perspective is that management, as we know it, is perfectly designed, but only for fighting yesterday's problems. And if we were being less generous, we would argue that even in the early 20th century when management was 'invented' (and designed), it failed even then at addressing important issues in the operating environment, let alone in valuing human dignity and the need for authenticity.

While management is defined in a number of different ways, there have been some clear and consistent basic terms that have spanned the period during which management has been formally studied (starting in the late 1800s). These identified the job of management as involving the following key activities (by Henri Fayol[1]):

1 forecasting;

2 planning;

3 organizing;

4 commanding;

5 coordinating; and

6 controlling.

Practically we might think of these tasks relating to the determination of budgets, the process of cost control, the way people are deployed, the timing and scheduling of activities, the way in which people are motivated to deliver their work, the process of accounting for performance at individual, task and divisional levels, the way people are developed, the mechanisms for limiting and enabling certain activities and behaviours, the way corporate messages are cascaded and so on.

Over the years, while it is clear that there has been the emergence of forms of management that have emphasized workplace democracy, for example, there has also been a continuation and growth of processes that have sought to do the opposite; to standardize activities and provide scripts specifying how people should work. Similarly, while there has been a growth in the sophistication of the tools and techniques that managers can now reach for in terms of how they might, for example, influence others, flex their style or motivate people, it has all been in aid of how to direct, coordinate and organize better. And so despite all that has happened, and despite the maturation of the discipline, the fundamental intent and practice of management remains more or less as it was a century ago. A good manager 'gets things done'. A good manager 'doesn't go over budget'. A good manager 'delivers the outputs for which they are accountable'. A good manager 'keeps everything going to plan'. These aphorisms have remained the same since management began.

And so, what if they aren't right? What if, at the very least, they need re-evaluating to see if they still apply? What if they are part of the problem when it comes to working successfully in a modern operating environment? And particularly for the purposes of this study, what if they restrict or block authenticity? It seems like a reasonable enough argument to test.

At the outset of this book we trailed a number of reasons why management might be seen as out of step with the modern business environment. These include:

● the current need for agility and flexibility (in a turbulent and 'slushy' environment), as compared to a management ethos that orientates towards uniformity, predictability and control;

- the current need for all eyes to be on the changing external environment (technology, competition, socio-cultural shifts etc), as compared to a management ethos that is typically focused inwardly, and about getting done what is on the plan;

- the current need for diversity of opinion and fresh perspectives to deal with new and novel circumstances, as compared to a management ethos that relies on deference and compliance to dominating methods or approaches;

- the current need for innovation and creativity which requires space, time and provocation to think differently, as compared with a management ethos of limiting 'distracting' behaviours/activities that reduce productivity; and

- the current need for high quality and insightful learning so that organizations can effectively anticipate and adapt to rapidly changing circumstances, as compared to management that is, in every way, about execution.

Related to these considerations are other issues that might cause us to question the current conceptions of management and leadership. By definition, leadership cannot be said to have happened until there are followers. Leaders need followers. A huge proportion of the literature on leadership is based on this *a priori* assumption, and much of the guidance on the topic is focused on how to influence people, how to mobilize support, how to motivate others, how to persuade, how to inspire, how to sell ideas, how to align people behind your intent, how to change behaviour, how to communicate your vision, how to tell the story of the organization, how to harness talent in service of your vision, how to coach, how to suggest, nudge, invite, cajole, insist, coerce and a hundred other ways to create followership. We would even go so far as saying that the vast majority of advice you will see written down about management or leadership involves this single idea.

We believe that there is something deeply wrong with all of this. It is not that this doesn't reflect a need within business, or that there is no merit in being good at getting people to follow you. It is that in the process of getting people to follow your agenda, you are doing just that. You are moving people away from whatever their priorities and aspirations might otherwise be, to what yours are. And what follows from this, in terms of where responsibility then sits, is the interesting part. We would suggest that the more effective leaders are at getting their people to follow *their* ideas, the greater risk they then carry that their followers won't feel a sense of ownership of the ideas and actions that arise. And just because they might use ever more sophisticated means of persuasion, the risk remains.

There are a host of responses that we can observe when people are obliged to act in accordance with someone else's priorities or aspirations, particularly if they don't match their own. We see instances where people will do the 'bare minimum' and where people will go 'through the motions'. We see examples of 'consent and evade' where workers give the impression of consent but in actual fact find ways to avoid and evade what is asked of them. We even see what we call 'malicious compliance' where a point is made of strictly, and to the letter, following the orders of management with the intention of proving that the order is wrong or inappropriate or just won't work. All of these reactions illustrate that securing followership is not the same as securing ownership of, or responsibility for, the actions that are required.

When we consider this in the broader organizational context where formal power already resides with people higher up in the organizational system, we see other dynamics. Deferential systems within organizations often serve to reduce responsibility that is felt by people 'at the bottom' for those decisions that are taken by what is often a small group of people 'at the top'. The dynamics that are at play produce a situation where:

- the deferrer is cast in a passive, rather than an active, role;
- reliance is placed on the knowledge of one person (the leader), rather than leveraging the intelligence and insight of both people (the leader and the follower);
- dependency on the deferred to (the leader) is created;
- the conditions for blame are established; and
- the responsibility from the person that should enact the decision (the follower) is displaced to the person that is least directly affected by the decision (the leader).

Illustrating this dynamic in the relationship between a doctor and a patient we can see how these might operate:

When we defer to others we simultaneously transfer some, and often all, of the responsibility to them, as it relates to the decision or action taken. For example, when we defer to a doctor on the best way to reduce our blood pressure, we hand over some of the responsibility for this solution to the doctor. And if we were to find that in taking the suggested steps or the medicine as prescribed, our blood pressure was not lowered, we might feel justified in directing some of our dissatisfaction for this outcome to the doctor. We would, in part, hold the doctor responsible for this failure.[2]

So this might cause us to pause for a moment on the question of where responsibility sits in the exercise of leadership. But there is also the question of what learning arises from following the leader. Earlier we spoke of the psychologist Carl Rogers who was clear that learning is at its most valuable when it is self-acquired. By this he means that we learn best when we have had the opportunity to discover for ourselves what matters most, what works best, what warrants greatest effort and so on. Being told, or even being persuaded of, what to do, removes from us and denies us the need to work out and learn for ourselves. You can be told how to drive a car. You can have it explained to you what all of the levers, dials and instruments do. You can have the workings of the combustion engine explained to you. But it is only when you sit in the driver's seat, and when you put your own foot on the accelerator and your own hand on the steering wheel that learning really happens. We learn most when we are facing and grappling with how to solve the challenges in front of us. If someone else tells us what our next move should be and we are obliged or motivated to comply, the opportunity to consider alternatives is removed along with the opportunity to fully appreciate why this is the right course of action. In an age where there is a premium on learning and the ability to learn, it is clear that we need to re-think the offer that leadership makes.

To make a final observation about the 'wisdom' of leadership, as currently enacted, we start with a question, namely – how many leaders does it take to run an organization? This is not the sort of question you hear being asked very often but, in theory, it should be possible to answer it. Within organizations we have people that we call and would recognize as being leaders (Category A). By implication, there are people in organizations that we would not call or recognize as being leaders (Category B). So the question is, how many/what proportion of people should be in Category A and what proportion should be in Category B? What would be your answer to this? Would it be 1 per cent in category A? Might it be 5 per cent? In a large organization employing, let's say, 40,000 people, if it was 1 per cent this would equate to 400 leaders. If your answer were 5 per cent this would suggest around 2,000 leaders. Does this seem a lot or too few?

Most (if not all) organizations have a top management team, typically comprising 6–10 people and it would be safe to assume that we would think of them as being in Category A. Many organizations have what they might describe as a senior group that comprises a number of people in the level below the top management team. For example, some organizations define a 'Top 200' group. It would seem appropriate to include these within Category A. While beyond this it becomes rather unclear, it is perhaps fair to assume that leadership is typically the responsibility of a small proportion of the organization and in fact if it involved very many people, we might then worry about the clarity, singularity and achievability of purpose that the organization could pursue.

The difficulty of leadership being the domain of the few is that important decisions are similarly shaped by the views and ideas of the few. Problems can arise when this occurs in deferential organizational cultures that operate on the working assumption that the judgements and decisions of those higher up the system should be accepted. There are a number of ways in which leadership of this sort generates difficulties. We have talked about the problem of the transfer of responsibility and the risk of 'consent and evade', but we also see leadership in these terms as having a deleterious effect in creating 'them and us' cultures. The diversity of voices, ideas and solutions that might otherwise flow through the organizational system become muted and in their place can be found a narrow band of judgements asserted by the most deferred to in the organization (the leadership). The more deference there is, the narrower the band of judgements upon which organizations rely.

And as for governance and ethical business, as discussed in Chapter 5 on the freedom to speak, systems of deference have for far too long enabled critical and influential decisions to remain unchecked and unchallenged because the decision-makers are treated with high levels of deference. With examples ranging from Enron/Andersen to the Global Financial Crisis to the UK Members of Parliament expenses scandal to the fascinating instance of the CEO of an Indian company that literally invented thousands of non-existent employees to strengthen the company's figures,[3] we see how deference insulates decision-makers against appropriate challenge.

To our question *how many leaders does it take to run an organization?* we might be left with a quandary. On the one hand, and with the problems of leadership ringing in our ears, we might challenge the value of leadership at all, at least in its current incarnation. On the other hand, we might argue that rather than a select, small group of leaders, we should instead look to significantly broadening the leadership pool. Whichever way we cut it, our proposition is that we need to revisit management and leadership, and we need to do so in such a way that will address the schism ('Solomon's Dilemma') discussed earlier. If authenticity can be placed at the heart of this new management movement we believe that individuals and organizations have an enormous prize waiting for them.

The 5 'A's management task

In this section we propose a framework for thinking about the task of management. Let us be clear that any role that we might play is a 'construction', whether it is a construction of a manager, a teacher or a barista in a coffee shop. There isn't a comprehensive instruction booklet for any role that we might take. There isn't a script that we should follow. The role of manager, for example, doesn't exist until it is inhabited and brought to life by someone. The way we do this will necessarily depend on the individual concerned. We find ourselves confronted by an almost infinite set of choices about how we are going to *be* in the role, and how we are going to manifest ourselves in the role. And so the way in which people 'manage' is individual, it is situational and it is a moment-to-moment dynamic process of construction. This dynamic interpretation, in this instance of the role of manager, is one way in which we might build in flexibility and agility to cope with changing circumstances.

With this in mind, we offer to managers a set of ideas and resources, that we describe as the '5 'A's management task' (Table 8.1 recaps). These, we hope, will inform and add to this process of construction. They are founded on the idea that authenticity needs to be seen as an important component of our working lives, and managers can make a meaningful contribution to this and to organizational success. In some respects this will be about 'getting out of the way' to allow others to step up to the job. In others, it will be about raising the quality of conversation that occurs between managers and managed. But it is essential that managers apprehend these ideas in a way that honours and leverages their own authenticity.

TABLE 8.1 The 5 'A's management task of authenticity

	Focus	Management role descriptor
1	Authenticity	Freedoms fighter
2	Adaptation	Head of learning and development
3	Alignment	Interpreter
4	Accountability	Accountability steward
5	Action	Occasional interventionist

There are five elements to the 5 'A's management task, each of which include a focus for attention, for example 'adaptation', and a corresponding role, such as 'head of learning and development'. The roles, and the way they are described, are deliberately imaginative and should be thought of as creative provocations to help the process of construction.

Authenticity and the role of freedoms fighter

In the role of Freedoms Fighter we are of course referring to the Freedoms and Authenticity model outlined earlier, and the encouragement that managers should bring this to life.

But the sentiment of a Freedoms Fighter is meant seriously, and this is because the weight of pre-existing expectations on managers regarding what managers should do will require some challenge and will entail some resistance. Perhaps too because the idea of management and creating freedom can seem something of a contradiction in terms. While the argument is clear and the benefits of authenticity that will arise for individuals and organizations alike are equally persuasive, it will nevertheless take commitment, creativity and persistence on the part of managers to inspire this change. We propose three key areas of attention for modern managers:

- role modelling authenticity;
- removing the blockers to authenticity; and
- a focus on 'min spec' management.

Role modelling authenticity

The 'shadow' that managers and leaders cast is a powerful resource in the right hands. The words, actions and behaviours of senior people are a source of great interest in an organization and can become quickly amplified, magnified and (sometimes disproportionately) imbued with meaning across and beyond an organization. An inspirational speech by a manager or even an unexpected moment of vulnerability can have positive effects on how people might perceive managers. Alternatively, one false slip of the tongue or even an unintended remark can be quickly taken, interpreted and ricocheted around the organization creating havoc in its wake.

The shadow that managers cast has an impact not only on how we perceive them, but also how we then might behave. There is a role modelling effect to the conduct of senior people that refers to a tacit assumption that if it's ok for my manager to do this, then it must be ok for me also. In the context of authenticity, it can be enormously liberating if managers are willing to take the risk involved in exhibiting greater levels of authenticity; dress more authentically, speak more authentically, operate more authentically and so on. As well as reaping the benefits personally from doing this (and by implication for the organization too), the benefits of managers showing authenticity are multiplied across the team, the area and beyond. The manager can be a powerful and efficient force in raising authenticity in an organization.

It is at this point where we might imagine a tension arising for a manager seeking to be authentic while at the same time feeling obliged to act in more traditional managerial ways. For an organization that values authenticity this tension is less likely to arise, but in organizations that still hold on to the idea that managers should control, direct, standardize, constrain and organize people and their work, this tension may be felt more acutely. Like most change, this entails a renegotiation of pre-existing norms, conventions, expectations and obligations. Perhaps our greatest ally in this process is what we might call 'social sense making', by which we mean that managers should engage in a participatory process of sense making that follows on from any movements towards authenticity that they may make. In doing this there are two important actions, to:

- narrate/articulate the change (explain the thinking behind the change); and

- engage openly, and often, in conversation about what it means for others.

Let's take an example of a boss who decides that in order to be more authentic they would like to engage more directly with the people in their area – something that reflects their own preference in terms of personal style. In doing this they take the decision to operate, unlike their peers, without an executive assistant who until that point had been the 'gatekeeper' of their diary. They do this because they believe that there should be no factors limiting access to them or processes that signal that it is hard to get time with the boss. Furthermore, they decide to move from their private office to sit in an open plan part of the building with people from their area but also other areas, to further underline the importance of free-flowing dialogue, unrestricted access and cross-divisional conversation. And finally, they decide to conduct all of their senior team meetings in open forum with observation from people at all levels strongly encouraged by the boss. These changes in behaviour would most likely give rise to a lot of conversation and speculation among teams, executive assistant, peers and so on.

Following the two simple rules above, our encouragement would be that the boss should first offer a narrative that explains their change in behaviour; perhaps something that explains that they feel more comfortable being able to spend unscheduled time with their teams, and the importance they give to people genuinely being involved in organizational decision-making. Secondly, the boss should deliberately seek to engage in, and encourage, 'social sense-making' about how others see this and how they are affected by it. We might think of this example as illustrating well the three freedoms of the Freedom to Operate, the Freedom to Speak and the Freedom to Actualize. Importantly though it is the second of these (the Freedom to Speak) which is absolutely essential. And so if part of the narrative and discussion that follows includes a recognition of how authenticity is central to the shift in behaviour, then those that observe this will not simply see the particular manifestation of the manager's behaviour, but the significance of what underpinned it in the first instance, ie the expression of authenticity. It is in this that is contained the power of role modelling.

Removing the blockers to authenticity

The Hawthorne experiments of the 1930s conducted by Elton Mayo underscore the effect that managers can have on workers. First set up to determine the impact of different lighting conditions (among other factors) on employee productivity, the experiments in Western Electric Hawthorne factory near Chicago revealed some surprise results. While initial results appeared to show that levels of employee productivity improved when lighting levels were increased, it seemed also that other variations to lighting conditions (including reducing levels) also had a positive effect on productivity. Subsequent analysis, combined with further experimentation with Harvard Business School, concluded that the very process of paying attention to workers (in this case to the subjects of the experiment) increased productivity. The phenomenon came to be called the 'Hawthorne Effect'. Its greatest contribution may have been to the fields of psychology and social research, and not to the field of employee engagement per se, but contained within this work were influential ideas about how managers direct their attention to employees and the beneficial effects of this.

In the context of this work, as managers pay attention to the worker's pursuit of authenticity, and in doing so communicate the importance they (the managers) attribute to it, the more likely we are to see levels of authenticity increase. This positive attention in itself helps to bring oxygen to the work of authenticity. But there are other ways in which managers can come to its aid, including seeking to remove the blockers standing in the way. We have already discussed one potential blocker, namely the behaviour that managers themselves model. But we also encourage managers to search out, pinpoint and neutralize other barriers to authenticity, particularly those associated with the three freedoms discussed earlier. Impediments to authenticity can take many forms but typically involve one or more of the following:

- Resource barriers, eg money, space, technology, time etc: this has particular relevance to the Freedom to Operate, but also for the other freedoms. Managers, for example, are able to redirect resources to facilitate different ways of doing business, they are able to create forums and time for deeper discussions to take place, and they are able to draw upon technology to facilitate different working practices. Consistent though with the philosophy underpinning this model, is the idea that authenticity should be pursued and reached for by individuals, with managers standing on the side-lines and removing barriers where appropriate. An example of this appears in our earlier case study of Timpson, the key cutting and shoe repairing company (see p 62). At one of their stores in London, located near an Embassy, one of the team noticed that they were increasingly attracting enquiries about photocopying services. The individual concerned undertook some enquiries which revealed that the Embassy had no provision for people to copy documents in support of visa and passport applications. He then invested some of the funds of the store in a standard copier and pretty soon had recouped the initial investment and was also generating a healthy sum towards earning his own monthly bonus. What facilitated this imaginative and entrepreneurial scheme was the organizational commitment to allow the Freedom to Operate combined with the support of managers to make funds available, to allow them time for the individual concerned to undertake their research and to show trust in the individual.

- Cultural barriers: this refers to the constraining effect of well-established cultural norms and conventions, or even the wider cultural position on exhibiting authenticity in an organization.

Managers can, for example, unblock assumptions that have become norms by offering alternative narratives that 'buck the trend' or by demonstrating different behaviours. One example of this is the impressive reframe that is offered by Jón Gnarr, the Mayor of Reykjavik, who adopts a highly unconventional approach to the work of being a Mayor. The fascinating style of Jón Gnarr warrants a book in its own right but for our purposes it is worth noting that he is extremely empowering in his dealings with others, he is deliberately playful and at times surreal in his interactions (to deliberately break the routine of bureaucratic processes). Unlike most Mayors his style of dress is very casual, he speaks with a striking degree of honesty and exhibits no difficulty with showing vulnerability with others. Examples that illustrate this approach include occasions on which Jón Gnarr has famously come to work dressed as Star War's legend Obi-Wan Kenobi, the way in which he personally administers his own Facebook page giving unprecedented access to his private life and thoughts, and the ease with which he speaks with people who meet him. The combined effect of this managerial approach is powerful and liberating for many around him who too seek to gain authenticity in their work.

- Approval barriers: this has particular relevance to the Freedom to Operate and managers have the opportunity to provide assistance in advising on, and in some instances lifting, barriers that might otherwise be too daunting for workers lower down the system.

- Self-limiting barriers: these could relate to a number of factors ranging from low levels of confidence to assumed (rather than actual) barriers to change. The 'un-blocking' work that managers might engage in here could take the form of coaching and mentoring, or might involve providing management 'cover' of one sort or another to lend some protection to workers trying new approaches or stepping up their level of dialogue.

- Rule rigidity barriers: rules and protocols appear in very many ways, from the way in which meetings are held and the formalities of when people are allowed to speak, to the processes for getting decisions made. It is our view that rules serve an invaluable purpose in protecting the organization and its people, and in guiding conduct. But there is often a point for many organizations where rules take on a life of their own, where they might become too rigid or become adrift from their original intent. Managers should play close attention to this area not least because in the rapidly changing 'slushy' environment that we are currently in, rules that aren't flexed or adapted to the circumstances will hold an organization back.

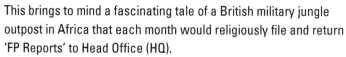

A tale of rule rigidity

This brings to mind a fascinating tale of a British military jungle outpost in Africa that each month would religiously file and return 'FP Reports' to Head Office (HQ).

These would arrive on time every month showing daily figures for the report, which were then faithfully transferred at HQ to a standing FP report kept as a permanent record. One day these reports stopped arriving with HQ and a reminder was immediately sent to the outpost to make staff there aware that they had failed to file their return. This was an unexpected and important breach in process. Some days passed and still no returns were submitted. A stronger missive was despatched to the outpost and only to be met again by silence.

Eventually HQ sent a senior member of staff to the outpost to personally investigate what had happened. An enraged senior officer took a more junior officer to task seeking a good reason why the reports had failed repeatedly to appear despite numerous reminders. The junior officer attempted to explain but his voice cracked as he spoke and the senior officer, now red in the face with anger, couldn't hear him. 'What did you say man? Speak up!' The junior officer lent forward and attempted again to explain himself 'Sorry sir, the lads and I were having a bit of a joke'. Again his voice broke half way through his sentence. The senior officer stiffened 'What the hell do you mean, it was a joke. These reports could make the difference between life and death, explain yourself'. The junior officer caught between the two emotions of unadulterated fear and near hysterics plucked up the courage and spoke to the senior officer 'The FP reports sir!' he started. 'It was just a joke. We were counting the number of flies that stuck to the flypapers. And we'd send them to HQ as FP reports.' As if to hammer the final nail into his own coffin the junior officer finished with, 'It does get a bit boring around here sir.'

A final observation about the 'unblocking' contribution that managers can make is taken from the work of Abraham Maslow and in particular his model of the hierarchy of needs (Figure 8.1).

This model can be used to think about some first order requirements that can stand in the way of authenticity. In the workplace, we might imagine a scenario where individuals look, for example, to exercise greater Freedom to Operate. Let's imagine that they have good managers that have made resources available for them to do so, or managers that have even tackled some of the cultural barriers that stand in the way. While all of this might help, if workers are fearful for their job security (ref: the 'need for safety' level of the model), or they are new to an organization with few friendship groups (ref: the 'need for belonging/love' level), then their ability to reach out for this freedom (F2O) or for other freedoms, may be severely hampered. At one level therefore, we might think of managers as being well placed to address, and where appropriate dispel, many of these concerns or myths that generate insecurities, in doing so this would create a safer environment for important risk-taking and experimentation to take place. We do not propose though that this is done in a parental or protectionist manner, as workers are adults and should be treated as such. However, as managers typically have access to information, for example, that will enable workers

FIGURE 8.1 Maslow's Hierarchy of Needs (1943)

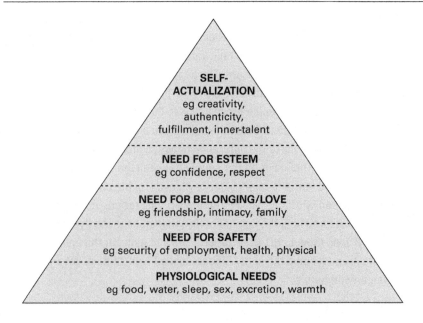

to understand the fuller picture and state of an organization at any given time, this will allow individuals to confront any concerns they might have.

It is useful to bear in mind that we can approach this model from both a positivist and a constructivist viewpoint. From a positivist perspective we find ourselves dealing with what we might regard as the objective facts or truth of a situation, and in doing so treat the consequences that arise as inevitable and a logical conclusion. In this sense the needs identified in Maslow's model might objectively be thought of as being satisfied or not, and if they are not we can observe the consequences that arise. For example, in an organization where financial rewards are under pressure and remuneration levels have been held still for some time, we might observe that workers will experience a loss of self-esteem and feel less job security (these are lower level requirements in Maslow's model that may stand in the way of the pursuit authenticity).

However, from a constructivist perspective this seemingly objective assessment of the situation can be viewed (or 'constructed') in a number of ways, and managers, as well as workers, have a role to play in this. So, a manager might focus attention on the broader context of other organizations facing similar wage freezes, they might give attention to the possibilities for change ushered in by tighter circumstances, or they might see this as a time when people can pull together. In doing so, we might then apprehend, in a different way, the needs identified by Maslow, and the extent to which they are met in individual circumstances. In constructivist terms this is not to suggest that managers pretend the situation is different from what it really is, or that we somehow misrepresent the truth. From the constructivist viewpoint the situation only has the 'truth' that we project onto it and there will always be competing accounts of a given situation and what it means.

We believe that this is the kind of managerial 'work', of looking in different ways at barriers to exercising freedoms, and ultimately to authenticity, that can help workers to make progress. At the very least managers can play a truly powerful role in getting these topics onto the table for discussion and facilitating meaningful discussions, and in subjecting different constructions to analysis.

A focus on 'min spec' management

Brenda Zimmerman, Professor of Strategic Management at the Schulich School of Business at York University in Toronto, proposes the use of what she calls a 'min spec' requirements strategy for managers that can leverage better results, build capabilities and bring about a transformation in how business is done.

With this approach leaders are asked to do the hard thinking and due diligence in specifying for their people a very small number of well chosen requirements in tackling key challenges. These are not minimum specifications in the sense that they refer to a low standard, rather, they are a deliberately pared down set of directions that release innovation and possibilities that otherwise might not have been imagined. One example of this approach is a 'min spec' referring to patient safety used by the Missouri Baptist Hospital that specifies that a) fix what you can, b) tell what you have fixed and c) report what you cannot. Another example developed by Ritz Carlton Hotels which, after considerable deep thinking that the final 'spec' can only hint at, was a specification that stated a) all employees will respond to the needs of their internal and external customers, and b) any employee who receives a customer complaint owns the complaint until resolved.

This concept of management fits well with the Freedoms Model and the principles of authenticity. By applying min spec requirements employees are afforded important degrees of latitude in determining how best to implement the rules. As this happens they bring their ideas, their skills and more of themselves to the task. The challenge for managers is to devise the min spec rules relevant to their area of responsibility. A starting point for this can be for managers to look at the existing rules in operation in a given area of work, to determine where opportunities might lie to reduce them. Managers might look to challenge the rules that are in place, perhaps asking questions such as:

- Can desired outcomes be achieved without following specific rules? Does this provide us with an opportunity to remove or refine existing rules?
- If other rules are met, but this one (the rule being looked at) is violated, can desired outcomes still be achieved? Does this provide us with an opportunity to remove or refine the rule?
- Can any blanket rules be used in fewer instances (for example, with procurement arrangements can across-the-board blanket rules be reserved for higher value purchases only?)
- How might existing rules be simplified?
- Are there opportunities to try out the application of fewer, more streamlined, min spec rules?

Beyond these suggestions, it is the underlying principle that is of greatest value to the pursuit of authenticity discussed here. Rather than managers looking to be prescriptive, this approach favours creatively reducing the constraints under which we operate, while firmly and clearly inspiring behaviour in a small number of important ways. The management work to do here may require application, but is hugely significant.

Adaptation and the head of learning and development

By definition, as organizations introduce the Freedoms Model, a greater range of possibilities and perspectives will be explored; as the Freedom to Operate is exercised, new ways of doing business will be developed. As the Freedom to Speak is enacted, new ideas and viewpoints will be shared in the organization. As the Freedom to Actualize is claimed, greater self-awareness will be achieved along with new apprehensions of the organization's value and purpose. You can almost hear the new level of buzz to be found in an organization of this sort.

Central though to all of these is the role of learning and adaptation. In fact, the Freedoms Model by design is an engine for continuous learning, something we believe, in this turbulent operating environment that organizations need to get good at.

We have talked already about the learning that sits with individuals exercising the different freedoms, but for managers too this is a critical role, and one that we suggest deserves much more attention than it is often given. With this in mind we invite each and every manager to think of themselves as the head of learning and development for their area of responsibility. Framing the management role in this way puts the focus on some key tasks:

- building the capabilities of individuals to keep pace with the challenges found when enacting the Freedom to Operate, Speak and Actualize;
- capturing the learning that arises from exercising the Freedom to Operate, Speak and Actualize;
- sharing the learning arising from exercising freedoms, in an intelligent and useful way (with other parts of the business, up the management line, and as a reflection back to individuals involved);
- drawing learning in from outside the division/organization to stimulate and inform the enactment of the three freedoms; and

- supporting small experiments and trials in all areas of the Freedoms Model.

Learning and development in organizations typically takes a number of forms ranging from formal training courses to on-the-job mentoring (and much in between), and our framing of this role is deliberately inclusive of all these options. There are both symbolic and practical merits of managers seeing themselves as central to this.

Symbolically, this interest in learning in itself offers an encouragement for workers to offer new ideas and experiment with them. These ideas might as easily be focused on holding more meaningful conversations with colleagues in the business, as they are about delivering more effective customer service. Managers showing curiosity and a keenness to learn from the outcomes, is a powerful form of encouragement. We have already spoken about this but it is worth underlining the point that learning, and the ability to adapt, is one of the most important capabilities that organizations need to master. While learning was always important, the pace of change in the operating environment means that what worked for this month, may not work for next month, and constant learning is required for us to act on this. Moore's Law is one particular illustration of this point.

Back in 1965 Gordon Moore, the co-founder and Chair Emeritus of the Intel Corporation, published an article in *Electronics Magazine*. In it he made a stunning statement about the growth of technology. He predicted that every 18 months the processing speed of microchips, that we find in our computers, cars, fridges etc would double (specifically, the number of transistors that can be placed on an integrated circuit board would double), and over the same period the cost of acquisition would halve. It was an incredible prediction and as the decades have passed it has caused considerable consternation simply because of its continued accuracy. As we look around us we can see and touch this pace of technological change, and at the same time our organizations look at ways to adopt new technologies more quickly and more successfully than their competition.

The 'swine flu' pandemic is another example of this phenomenon of change. In 2009 when it happened it was, for many, a truly frightening occurrence. With hindsight we know that the number of deaths did not continue to rise at the rate it did in the first few months. By the end of April 2009 there had been seven confirmed deaths, a month later this had risen to 99 deaths, another month later 313, then by month four 1,126 deaths.[4] If it had continued to increase at this rate, we might have expected something in the region of 181,000 deaths in the following four months to November 2009, affecting every country in the world. In practice, deaths rose and then fell to 8,450 and although still a significant and regrettable number, thankfully did not match the initial worst case projections. The point of this example is that at the time we of course didn't have the benefit of hindsight but were required to make important decisions and learn from the data in the moment, and at a rapid rate. Learning is a priority capability that we need to improve to thrive in the modern era, and managers that take this seriously will signal to others the importance that this holds.

Practically, there is a great deal of assistance that managers can provide as people embrace the Freedoms Model. Taking the Freedom to Operate as an example, each time that an individual takes steps to creatively challenge their Absolute Freedom to Operate (AF2O) or their Residual Freedom to Operate (RF2O), they will create learning about the organization, their role, the intended outcomes of their work, what is valuable in what they do and so on. Similarly, as individuals feel empowered to track down areas for improvement they will encounter challenges and see breakthroughs that may need support and 'unblocking' by managers. In all of this learning will both be required and produced. The manager's role is to help capture, understand, disseminate, catalyse and piece together the learning in support of the individual, and for others too. If we pause here for a moment though we can see the immense value that can be created when enacting the Freedom to Operate. As this happens, individuals find themselves working to understand, at a deep level, the purpose of their role and what counts as a good result. They will find themselves not only focused on their part of the business but as they deepen their understanding of what matters most, they will see more clearly the connections between what they and other parts of the business do. The sense of ownership that comes from this generates commitment and engagement, and the ideas that arise from this process will be the same ideas that keep the organization on its toes and able to survive and thrive.

An important practical offer that managers can make relates to supporting experiments or trials to test out new ways of doing business. A fascinating example of using trials is that of the work of the UK's Behavioural Insights Unit (also called the 'Nudge Unit'). Originally established in 2010 as a unit in the British Cabinet Office, and since constituted as a limited company, the Nudge Unit:

> Applies insights from academic research in behavioural economics and
> psychology to public policy and services. In addition to working with almost

> every government department [the Unit] works with local authorities, charities, NGOs, private sector partners and foreign government, developing proposals and testing them empirically across the full spectrum of government policy.[5]

It has undertaken a range of projects that have included helping unemployed people find work, improvements in timeliness in the payment of court fines, and work to determine the impact of alcohol unit pricing to tackle binge drinking. Drawing their ideas from the disciplines of social psychology, economics and sociology, and in particular the work of Nobel Prize winner Richard Thaler and Cass Sunstein, adviser to the US President, the Unit has made some breakthrough results. For example, with their work on organ donation they have successfully encouraged 100,000 more British citizens to carry organ donor cards. This was achieved through relatively small, but significant changes to the wording in online processes for people renewing drivers' licences. The unit has claimed savings of hundreds of millions of pounds (sterling) through innovations in the work of government such as this. Of particular interest in their approach has been the emphasis given to experiments and specifically randomized controlled trials (RCTs), an approach that the unit argues should be used more often, and more systematically:

> Randomized controlled trials (RCTs) are the best way of determining whether a policy is working. They have been used for over 60 years to compare the effectiveness of new medicines... However, they are not yet common practice in most areas of public policy.[6]

The approach follows a test, learn and adapt methodology, which situates experimentation, in a particularly managed and scientific sense, at the heart of the work. The randomized process allows learning to be derived from an experiment while holding still, and making ready for comparison, the results from 'normal' processes:

> Let us imagine that we are testing a new 'back to work' programme which aims to help job seekers find work. The population being evaluated is divided into two groups by random lot. But only one of these groups is given the new intervention... The other... is given the usual [job seeker] support. [7]

A specific example of this design, and the use of the test, learn and adapt methodology is shown here:

Case example: Trials to improve the payment of court fines

The UK Courts Service and the Behavioural Insights Team wanted to test whether or not sending text messages to people who had failed to pay their court fines would encourage them to pay prior to a bailiff being sent to their homes. The way this question was answered is a clear example of the 'test, learn, adapt' approach, and the concurrent testing of multiple variations to find out what works best.

In the initial trial, individuals were randomly allocated to five different groups. Some were sent no text message (control group), while others (intervention groups) were sent either a standard reminder text or a more personalized message (including the name of the recipient, the amount owed, or both). The trial showed that text message prompts can be highly effective with increases in payments varying from between a quarter and a third of cases (23–33 per cent) as a direct result of being sent reminder texts.

A second trial was conducted using a larger sample (N = 3,633) to determine which aspects of personalized messages were instrumental to increasing payment rates. The pattern of results was very similar to the first trial. However, the second trial gave confidence that not only were people more likely to make a payment on their overdue fine if they received a text message containing their name, but that the average value of fine repayments went up by over 30 per cent.

The two trials were conducted at very low cost: as the Courts Service was already collecting the outcome data, the only cost was the time for team members to set up the trial. If rolled out nationally, personalized text message reminders would improve collection of unpaid fines; simply sending a personalized rather than a standard text is estimated to bring in over £3 million annually. The savings from personalized texts are many times higher than not sending any text reminder at all. In addition to these financial savings, the Courts Service estimates that sending personalized text reminders could reduce the need for up to 150,000 bailiff interventions annually.

It is not proposed, necessarily, that individuals in the workplace, acting on the Freedom to Operate, should construct control trials such as these, rather that the convention of conducting experiments should be seen as an essential feature of organizational life; one that is driven by individuals and practically supported by managers. What we too often see in organizations is a very different approach to change that is instead characterized by the introduction of large scale change, introduced from above, and without the built-in scope for learning and adaptation. Not only does this approach deny the opportunity for real evaluation, but it very often fails to leverage the authentic support of people within the business, and it fails to benefit from the insights and instincts of workers engaged in the work on a daily basis.

More generally, managers presiding over experiments by workers exercising their Freedom to Operate may wish to bring resources and training to this work so that the best learning can be drawn from it. This may involve development and teaching that is reflective of an RCT approach, or it may be just to bring rigour and confidence to the work that individuals then take on.

So far we have emphasized the learning dimension to one of the freedoms, namely the Freedom to Operate. But of course this applies to all three freedoms and taking as another example, the Freedom to Actualize, we can see managers playing an important role in learning and adaptation here.

The Freedom to Actualize is an interesting example as it takes us on an arguably deeper and more personal journey, and so any form of assistance that managers might provide in this process requires skill, sensitivity and a trusting relationship. But also managers will be extremely well placed to offer insight in a number of areas. If we think of the work that the Freedom to Actualize involves we can see managers making a valuable contribution that includes:

- building the self-awareness of the individual concerned;

- providing insights into the meaning and value of the work done;

- identifying the conditions when an individual can be 'in flow';

- making sense of the values of the organization; and

- facilitating conversation about parts of an individual's personality or interests that are typically kept out of view.

Similarly, we might think of a manager engaging people in the obligations that arise as they exercise the freedoms, namely:

- the obligation to engage with the corporate messages and priorities of the organization so that freedoms are taken in full awareness of these;

- the obligation to honour the ethics and values of the organization when acting on freedoms;
- the obligation to proactively share the success or otherwise of acting on the freedoms;
- the obligation to undertake 'de-risking' activity when attempting new and novel approaches;
- the obligation to build understanding (and act on this) of the potential impact of changes and actions arising from freedoms; and
- the obligation to accept accountability for actions that arise from accepting freedoms.

While these obligations first and foremost sit with the individuals exercising freedoms, managers have a practical, supporting role to play with respect to learning.

All of the contributions that managers can make, discussed so far in this section, underline the elevation of status given to this role of 'head of learning and development'. To do this well requires a level of commitment that exceeds what is usually imagined for managers; this is about much more than the 'fire and forget' convention of putting people on training courses or holding a twice-yearly performance review discussion – it is a stronger and more important role. It is humanizing too and frames managers and workers not as connecting cogs in a machine but as people engaged in a shared endeavour; both on the same journey, fulfilling different functions and seeking to understand what they are trying to accomplish, how to do it better, why it matters, how it relates to life beyond work and so on.

Alignment and the role of interpreter

Making sense of organizational intent, at any one given point in time, is much more difficult than it may seem. For anyone within an organization there are the tasks that are immediately in front of him or her, and these provide the clearest practical manifestation of the organization's intent. But organizations are understandably engaged in anticipating and responding to external factors, and in an uncertain operating environment, this causes organizations to continually shift their priorities and reinterpret their intentions. Very few organizations are not involved in implementing major change of one form or another, and most are making change on multiple fronts. Here are some examples of organizations and the specific changes they are introducing:

- Barclays Investment Bank. In the wake of the 2008 Global Financial Crisis and the 2012 Libor scandal, the Investment Bank has set out to rebuild trust with customers and stakeholders through a large reinvention of its corporate values. This has seen, among other things, over 1,000 employees being trained as values educators and a cross-organizational programme of raising awareness and accountability-building for the new values.

- Australian Government Department of Human Resources (DHS). In 2011 the largest single Australian government department was created through the merger of five agencies namely Medicare, Centrelink, Child Support, Australian Hearing and CRS Australia. Alongside this the new organization has committed to radically reorienting its services towards the needs of citizens and doing so through significantly enhanced online provision. At the time of writing there is also the prospect that the DHS would be merged with the Australian Social Services Department.

- Greater Manchester Fire and Rescue Service. The Fire Service has been boldly working on a number of deep changes. In order to drive down the number of deaths caused by fires there has been a shift towards significantly more preventative activity (local education, installation of smoke alarms etc), combined with a greater emphasis on risk assessment in deploying resources. At the same time the service has faced government cuts in the order of 20 per cent of budgets that has impacted the entirety of the organization's operations. Finally it has made important moves towards finding alternative technological solutions to the remaining risks.

- Technip. Originally a Paris-based engineering company employing 100 people (1958), Technip grew and focused its operations on pipelines for the oil and gas industry, and is now a world leader for project management, engineering and construction for the energy industry, employing some 38,000 people. In the last three years alone it has grown by 16,000 people through a series of major acquisitions, it has firmly established its position in the energy space (not only oil and gas) and it has expanded the number of vessels it owns to 34 (including seven under construction).

For each of these organizations, we can see how the everyday tasks undertaken by employees might be influenced by these changes. But we can also see the difficulty of doing this interpretive work, for example:

- How should the role of the legal department in Barclays Investment Bank be changed by the organization's new values?
- How should workers in Medicare (supporting the provision of healthcare) work differently now that they are seated alongside people that work for Centrelink (supporting job seekers)?
- How should fire fighters that joined the service to put out fires make sense of their new role as educators?
- How should employees of the companies newly acquired by Technip understand their role in a larger organization?

This interpretive task is therefore important in its own right, but when we add into this the Freedoms Model that encourages workers to act, for example, with greater Freedom to Operate, there is a strong argument again for managers to help workers in understanding their corporate context – to connect together these two dynamic worlds. What this looks like for the manager is more than a simple cascade of corporate messages, as this would assume that little or no interpretation was required. Instead, we see managers as looking to press, poke and test the messages that emerge. We see them as getting beneath the words to understand the value that will be delivered through local adoption. We see them searching for the external factors that have prompted change in the first instance.

We also see that even where large-scale change or transformation is not under way, workers nevertheless need assistance in understanding the priorities that the organization gives to certain activities so that they can make informed judgements when exploring the Freedom to Operate differently. For example, in supermarkets we know that the speed with which checkout workers scan purchases through the till can have an impact on total sales. Higher performing supermarkets look to achieve 18 swipes per minute. If among the larger stores for example, average performance were to fall to say, 16 scans per minute, this would amount to hundreds of millions of pounds less revenue each year. Without this knowledge a worker may simply be told to work faster or talk less. Armed with this knowledge, a checkout worker can be clearer about the implications of decisions they make based on the Freedoms Model.

But this sharing and interpretation needs to work in multiple directions not just from the top down. As well as managers interpreting corporate messages for local application, as freedoms are exercised locally and experiments are developed, this needs to be interpreted, made sense of, and connected back to the corporate centre. And this should be shared laterally across the organization too, between like and unlike business units. For example, as lessons are learned about the Freedom to Actualize locally, managers should take it upon themselves to move these lessons out of the local area, for the benefit of others.

Managers can engage in a further act of interpretation and sense making by finding ways to articulate (or narrate) the purpose of the business so that individuals can then undertake their work authentically. We do not mean by this that managers should in some way seek to trick people into believing in a purpose for the business that is untrue; rather, we are describing a process of finding truths in the value and purpose of the business with which individuals can align their own values.

As we saw in the second chapter, emotional labour that is characterized by truly felt emotion is less damaging to health and more fulfilling for the individual than the kind of dissonant emotion that is manufactured as part of a service offering without bearing any relationship to what is truly felt by the employee.

This process of interpretation requires the manager to think deeply about the purpose and value of the organization and the roles within it. For example, a rather trite and superficial account of the purpose of the shoe repairers Timpson discussed earlier would be 'to make money', however if this was solely the case than no doubt their model would be much less complex and possibly less pleasant to read about. In fact they, as most businesses, are responding to some kind of human need and contained within this is a much more relatable truth. In this way, Timpson could be said to be providing a service that turns life's more mundane chores (key cutting, shoe repairs, etc) into an agreeable and friendly experience in order to improve the quality of life for customers. There is no 'Pollyanna' element to this interpretation as it drives both employee behaviour and customer loyalty and is a cornerstone of Timpson's success. Another truth about Timpson is the commitment it shows to the welfare of those who need a break in life. This is manifest in the level of publicity and support it gives to issues such as foster care for children, or prison rehabilitation programmes. Yet another is a pride in quality of service. These are all truths about the organization that are more readily discernible as fitting with the Freedom to Actualize. With the help of managers, individuals can find an interpretation of the meaning and value of their work that aligns with their values and enables them to be expressed through action.

A word of caution is advisable, and this is that managers should look at the impact of the organization as a whole and not ignore the less attractive impacts that may be present as this would entirely go against the whole idea of authenticity. For example, an organization that promotes animal welfare and yet causes widespread environmental destruction in its manufacturing processes would struggle to make a convincing case for the value that it is delivering to the animal world. This is an exercise that requires honesty and openness.

Managers may want to ask themselves the following questions when undertaking this piece of work.

- What is the value that we deliver to customers?
- What is the value that we deliver to the community?
- What makes us unique, eg history, commitment to high standards, service ethos etc?
- What am I not facing about our negative impacts?
- What is the human narrative about our organization/business?

A final word of caution about alignment

Learning environments, that are essential to the Freedom to Actualize and to creating agile organizations, thrive on experimentation, challenge and intellectual provocation. In order to drive learning, managers need to be sensitive to an overabundance of alignment within their organization that can lead to an orientation towards consensus building and a false security in the appropriateness of decisions (Groupthink also). This is an area where judgement will be needed to draw the line between 'just enough' alignment and 'too much'.

In this way, managers need to keep the tension in the system by encouraging challenge within decision-making processes and by finding new ways to frame issues. Constructive criticism and left field viewpoints can be stifled in the cozy warmth of consensus and blind spots can start to appear. Decisions can be settled upon without all of the issues at hand being fully engaged and the risk to organizations within this behaviour is plain to see.

In Professor Ronald Heifetz's words, managers wishing to keep, 'the jaws of the dilemma open', for as long as possible in order to fully engage with all the issues, may want to think about encouraging questions along these lines:

- What are the realities that we are not facing here?
- When would this not be a good idea?
- Have we heard from everybody who will be affected by this (proposition, initiative etc)?
- How about if we look at this from a different angle?
- What would others (Group X, Person Y) say about this if they were here?

Accountability and the role of steward

Accountability is a phrase widely used in business but rarely developed in its definition and meaning. It is often framed in terms of a concrete relationship between two or more parties where one party is accountable to another for the execution of a duty promised by the former. For example, if a customer service agent promises to get back the following day to a customer relating to their enquiry, they might be regarded as being accountable for that action. But in addition to this grounded description of accountability, we might also think of someone acting as if they were accountable to an abstract purpose or principle, for example, a principle of fairness. In these terms we can think of accountability as having practical or moral dimensions, but also having other qualities such as legal or social obligations in relation to the conduct of an individual. But missing from this is a recognition that not only can individuals be held accountable, but so can organizations. This is a useful and important starting point for our discussion of the managerial role of steward as this captures, among other things, the multi-directional nature of this task. Accountability needs to be exercised both in the way that an individual in an organization operates but also in the way that the organization operates with respect to its employees, its clients, its stakeholders and its values. We see managers as playing a central role to this.

Professor Mark Moore of Harvard's Kennedy School offers an extension to this idea that relates to the ability to judge performance and conduct: 'The idea of accountability as a moral ideal may also include a requirement that an actor make it easy for stakeholders to monitor the extent to which it has lived up to its promises.'[8]

This introduces some interesting notions about accountability that we might think of in three dimensions. Firstly, being held to account implies a need for evidence or a basis for which performance against a given standard can be judged. Secondly, an individual or organization that might provide information for these purposes is by definition demonstrating a degree of accountability. And thirdly, responsiveness to the expectations and demands of stakeholders is also an expression of accountability.

But to develop this further again, it is not sufficient to think of accountability as being purely objective in nature, and Moore argues that there are important questions to ask about the relationship between the social and objective establishment of accountability and the subjective experience:

There is lots of evidence from both corporate suites and mean streets that individuals will not necessarily feel or act in accord with socially constructed (and in that limited sense, objective) concepts of either moral responsibility or legal accountability.[9]

And so we observe that accountability can be thought of in some important ways:

- Accountability can be thought of as invoking a range of practical, moral, social, performance or legal obligations.
- People or organizations can be thought of as accountable for their actions.
- Accountability can be thought of in both objective and subjective terms.
- Being held to account requires evidence of performance against a given standard.
- Individuals or organizations that might provide information for the purposes of accountability are, by definition, demonstrating a degree of accountability.
- Responsiveness to the expectations and demands of stakeholders is also an expression of accountability.

A final element to this that is particularly relevant to the application of the Freedoms Model is the idea of personal accountability. We have discussed our philosophical framework for authenticity – highlighting that not only does the responsibility for authenticity reside with the individual (and not with someone else), but also so does the responsibility for the obligations that then arise. In other words as workers act upon their freedoms *they* are obliged to take responsibility for how this impacts on others, the organization's ambitions, values and so on. Our view of the manager's role is as follows: The manager's role is appropriately described as a 'Steward'. In this context the manager is not asked here to take over the responsibility for individual or organizational conduct or to manage the accountability process, but instead to act in ways that will preserve and care for the organizational environment. Our definition of the organizational environment includes the impact on customers, clients, stakeholders, and the law as much as it refers to the organization's internal goals, values, treatment of people and exercise of their authenticity. Stewardship of this kind needs to happen at the level of the manager, as managers are perfectly positioned between the corporate body and the individual worker.

Three levels of accountability

In the normal course of business, managers typically feel accountable for the results that have been handed down to them, which in turn they may delegate to their direct reports with corresponding accountabilities. This downward flow of accountability partially represents the proposal we make here but we suggest that three other accountabilities should also be enacted (Figure 8.2), that is:

- the need for managers to look upwards to hold the organization's leadership accountable for its conduct;
- the need for managers to hold the wider organization accountable, for example in its dealings with customers, stakeholders and so on; and
- the need for managers to look to the exercise of personal accountabilities as the three freedoms are exercised by individuals.

While this might appear to be quite a heavy undertaking for managers, this highlights in many ways the critical role that they play in supporting authenticity at both the individual and organizational level. This enhanced responsibility is often missing in organizational life but with it organizations will be much better placed to be authentic.

FIGURE 8.2 The three proposed dimensions of accountability for managers (in addition to business-as-usual accountabilities)

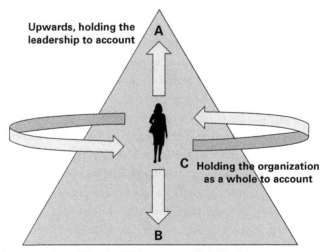

Furthermore, we might think of a number of high profile instances where acting on this commitment might have saved the reputation of organizations, kept them in line with their values, and in many instances saved them from serious financial consequences. High-profile examples might include the actions of Enron and their auditor's Andersen during the 2001 Enron scandal, the Tyco and Worldcom scandals in 2002, the HealthSouth financial scandal of 2003, the behaviour of banks in the lead up to the 2008 global financial crisis, the conduct of British Members of Parliament before the 2009 expenses scandal, the Jimmy Savile case and related BBC controversies of 2012, the Libor scandal of the same year, and the European horsemeat scandal of 2013 that saw 40,000 tons of beef recalled from stores, restaurants and supermarkets across Europe. In the vast majority of these cases, and those like them, managers (as well as others) were privy to knowledge about potentially inappropriate and inauthentic conduct of employees. A different set of obligations around accountabilities, if embraced, could have made a significant and positive impact on these and similar situations.

In exercising each of these accountabilities, we may encounter some practical challenges. Arguably, it is easier for a manager to hold to account their direct reports, than it is for them to hold their senior leaders to account, or for that matter to hold the organizational body to account. But this does depend on a number of factors:

- the degree to which the culture/systems of the organization are deferential;
- the extent to which the Freedom to Speak is embraced by all in the organization;
- the visibility afforded to the conduct of senior leaders in the organization (or the conduct of the organization as a whole); and
- the quality of the specific reporting and escalation mechanisms in place should formal action need to be taken.

With this in mind we can see that there are broader responsibilities that the organization needs to grasp if it is to utilize an accountability framework of this kind. We have spoken already about the importance of hastening the death of deference and also the value of establishing the Freedom to Speak (in Chapter 5) and both, in our view, remain top priorities for modern organizations. With regard to the transparency of conduct for senior leaders and the organization, this is an area that warrants attention. There are lessons to be learned from the public sectors across the world about how to address this, and in particular from the work of Charles Perrow (discussed shortly).

Freedom of information (also known as right to information) is one such example. Legislation has been implemented in over 90[10] countries worldwide introducing a 'right to know' legal process that enables citizens to obtain information and documents that pertain to the conduct of government business and to the use of taxpayers' money. Variations are present across countries in the way that this is implemented, but in general there are some clear principles that are commonly applied such as the requirement for the burden of proof to sit with the authority being asked, that is, it is not up to the enquirer to justify why they need the information, rather it is for the authority to disclose valid reasons (that can be subjected to scrutiny) should the requested information not be provided.

The very first law of this kind was enacted in Sweden in 1776, and while a small number of other countries passed similar legislation much later, for example the United States in 1966 (which became strengthened in 1976) and Australia and New Zealand in 1982, by 1990 only 14 countries had signed up to the right to information laws. But in the following 20 years, around four countries each year joined up to the arrangement. As of May 2012, some 5.5 billion[11] people live in countries that include in their domestic law an enforceable right, at least in theory, to obtain information from their governments.

This is a movement that is seeing governments around the world proactively, freely and often without agenda or sense of what is possible, making large datasets available to the public (which of course includes analysts, research bodies, academics etc) to encourage dialogue, openness and innovation. Ironically, the Wikileaks ethos in many ways fits well with the Transparency Agenda as pursued by an increasing numbers of governments, although it certainly pushes the limits of ambition.

A small example of this taken from India, relates to Sunder Nagri, an area to the north-east of New Delhi known for its slum dwelling and deprived living conditions. The story centres on the owner of a small local business, Noshe Ali, who had grown tired of the poor sanitation and sewerage in the area, as well as the government's unfulfilled promises to take action. Armed with a new law that required authorities, for a small fee, to disclose information about their activities and spending, he was able to reveal that there were in fact no plans at all to dig any sewers and improve local sanitation. With the bit in his teeth he challenged and worked with the capital's Chief Minister and eventually secured authorization of a budget and work commenced within a year. The results were as Noshe Ali had hoped: 'This place used to be dirty. There were lots of mosquitoes and many people caught disease. Now things are quite different.'[12]

The information law has been welcomed by members of India's poorest communities who have seen opportunities to find ways around obfuscation by state officials and to empower themselves in ways not previously enjoyed. But more than this, the new power balance has meant that individuals with limited access to funds but still needing services such as water connections, electricity, passports, driving licenses and so on, do not have to pay inequitable sums, or sometimes bribes, to receive services. Some have gone as far as to call the development a revolutionary act:

> When someone learns to use RTI [right to information], he almost becomes addicted to it. It's so powerful, it empowers the very ordinary citizen in a tremendous way.[13] (Arvind Kerjiwal, former Civil Servant)

Similar developments to this in the public sector at least for some countries are 'proactive disclosures' where senior officials will proactively make known their use of hospitality, travel, expenses and so on (through the web). This will be expressed to a level of details that might show, for example, who attended a lunch and when, the purpose, the venue, the cost and which parties paid.

Both approaches (FOI and proactive disclosures) make highly visible the conduct of employees in relation to a given topic and in doing so make an important contribution to exercising accountability.

With this in mind we turn to the notion of 'normal accidents' and the learning that can be derived from this. The phrase normal accidents was first coined by Yale Sociology Professor Charles Perrow in 1984 and refers to accidents that occur as a result of multiple and unexpected failures that are combined. Perrow's work is principally focused on complex technological systems although parallels can be drawn to other organizational and human systems. Perrow was not the first scholar to examine accidents in a new way. In many ways, he followed the work of the British sociologist Barry A Turner, who made a close study of 84 accidents in the United Kingdom. In 'Man-Made Disasters', published in 1979, Turner noted two phenomena that are found:

- Man-made disasters don't happen out of the blue. Typically, they have an incubation period, a time when unnoticed sets of problems begin accumulating.

- Relevant detail often is buried within a mass of irrelevant information. People don't go around with their eyes closed but as

Turner notes, 'A way of seeing is always also a way of not seeing.' In one instance, Turner found that memos that might have prevented a deadly rail accident went unread because they were regarded as 'flotsam' in the system.

While we are looking at accountability and authenticity, and not at complex technological systems or catastrophic failures, what can be drawn from the work of Perrow and Turner is an appreciation of two important factors:

- The need to pay attention to an accumulation of actions or events that might cause undesired outcomes.
- The importance of observation, data, and reporting, and in particular the value of fresh perspectives and 'different eyes' on the issue in order to overcome our routine ways of 'not seeing' (to separate the irrelevant data from the meaningful).

How this can be done will vary from organization to organization but this underlines in red ink the importance of all employees and particularly managers in seeing it as a priority to take accountability seriously, and the information engine that drives this.

In terms of the mechanisms available we might think of these as falling into two categories. The first we might think of as cultural mechanisms. By this we mean that in many organizations, particularly those where authenticity is enacted, it will be culturally normal for frank and straight discussions to be held about how business is being conducted. The mechanisms therefore are everyday conversation and dialogue and although sensitive and difficult matters might be discussed the organization is mature and adult in its behaviour; it is resilient enough to tackle the issues that might arise. Secondly we might think in terms of formal mechanisms that facilitate issues being confronted in situations where the culture is unlikely to, or unable to, take action. We have talked about formal mechanisms such as the freedom of information mechanism in the public sector. Another such formal mechanism is whistleblowing. As a mechanism this can be useful but research shows that care has to be taken.

In the wake of the scandals and fraudulent conduct of recent years, a Whistleblowing Commission was established in the UK. In coordination with Ernst & Young it released a report in 2013 that underlined the importance of designing whistleblowing processes that are effective:

> Recent scandals in many sectors, including banking, healthcare, construction and even in the media might have been prevented if it had been easier and safer

to speak up and whistleblowers had been listened to. It is time for companies and the regulators alike to take the problem seriously.[14]

The survey conducted by the Commission highlighted the concerns it had: 93 per cent of respondents said they have formal whistleblowing arrangements in place, but:

- one in three respondents think their whistleblowing arrangements are not effective;
- 54 per cent of respondents said they do not train key members of staff designated to receive concerns;
- 44 per cent of respondents confuse personal complaints with whistleblowing;
- 1 in 10 respondents say their arrangements are not clearly endorsed by senior management; and
- 1 in 10 respondents do not include procedures on how to protect a whistleblower, which is the main reason why a worker might not speak up.

And so the formal mechanisms that are in place, with whistleblowing as one such example, need intelligent design:

Confidentiality and protection of the whistleblower are key aspects of trust, as is demonstrating that a complaint will be taken seriously. A key feature is the need for adequately resourced and suitably experienced personnel being responsible for the triaging of reports.[15]

Finally, we see the accountability role that managers might play as their direct reports claim the three freedoms (to operate, to speak and to actualize) as an extension of what has already been said about other incarnations of accountability, namely:

- Managers should encourage and assist workers (exercising their freedoms) to proactively share information related to this. For example, as workers develop new ways of meeting their goals they should tell the story of this to colleagues.
- Managers should encourage workers to engage colleagues in discussion about the freedoms they claim and in doing so understand how this impacts on others.
- Managers should engage staff regularly in the meaning and importance of what they do, and the values that underpin this.

- Managers should work to remove systems of deference that otherwise restrict the flow of information and dialogue between levels. This along with other approaches will help to establish cultural mechanisms for bringing accountabilities to life.

- Managers should give their attention to the design or enhancement of formal mechanisms that will enable accountabilities to be exercised.

Action and the role of occasional interventionist

It may seem a little unusual to have action as the last item on this list of managerial responsibilities, and perhaps more surprising to have the role expressed as 'occasional interventionist'. This is because at the heart of the proposition to this book is that authenticity will arise through individuals taking responsibility for both enacting freedoms (F2O, F2S, F2A) while also taking responsibility for the obligations that arise. We developed this point further in terms of our Libertarian and Existentialist position, namely people are self-governing individuals who make choices and are responsible for them. Authenticity is rightly a concern for all, but it is for the individual to define it for themselves, to strive to attain it (should they choose to), and importantly to resist giving way to the temptation that it is the job of management to furnish it for them. My authenticity sits with me, yours with you, and it is not our belief that it is anyone's responsibility to find it or 'fix it' for someone else.

Consistent with this idea is the role of manager as one that does not step in and direct how people do their work, as this would run counter to our central argument. Contrary though to what might be imagined, we believe that in organizations where this principle is embraced you do not have workers that need telling what to do. You do not have individuals that side-step responsibility. You do not have people that feel that they cannot be themselves at work because their managers require them to be otherwise. The idea that workers cannot be trusted is reflected in Macgregor's managerial critique of the 1960s and captured through Theory X. This theory framed employees as inherently lazy and orientated towards work avoidance. Correspondingly management meant close supervision and the development of systems of control. Hierarchical structures with narrow ranges of responsibility were described along with motivational schemes that drew workers out of their inherent laziness and coercive mechanisms were applied when they didn't comply. This couldn't be further away from our experience of employees.

So, our position is absolutely clear on this, but we recognize that there will be times when managers will need to move from a position of facilitation, 'unblocking' and guidance to a more interventionist approach. This will be rare and in fact if this were to be a regular or increasingly frequent occurrence, we would suggest that there was something else at fault in the implementation of the system of freedoms. The circumstances that might trigger the need for closer involvement from managers could take a number of forms. Rather than provide an account of all possibilities, we wish to focus on three examples as follows:

- Example 1 – when a workplace is toxic.
- Example 2 – at times of crisis.
- Example 3 – when individual obligations related to the Freedoms Model are not being observed.

But we also want to ensure that managers go into this mode with their eyes open and so in the paragraphs that follow it is our aim to both highlight the value of decisiveness, and also to pose some provocations that will drive a more informed managerial response.

Managerial intervention: example 1 – when a workplace is toxic

The work of Gilbert, Carr-Ruffino, Ivancevich and Konopaske offers some useful insights into the variety of ways in which we might understand toxicity at work,[16] with toxic workplaces being toxic where (one or more of the following occur):

- Mediocre performance is rewarded over merit-based output.
- Employees avoid disagreements with managers for fear of reprisal.
- Personal agendas take precedence over the long-term well-being of the company.
- Leaders are constantly on edge and lose their tempers often.
- New leaders do not stay long and employee turnover is common.
- Employees are treated more like financial liabilities than like assets.
- Bosses routinely throw tantrums.

Interestingly the definitions provided here extend into the domain of managers as much as they do to the managed. Taking the first example of 'performance that is rewarded without merit' we glimpse an underpinning expectation placed on managers to be vigilant, sound in their judgements and above all fair. The consequence of not doing this can be thought of as toxic. Similarly, managers that 'throw tantrums', make workers feel fearful or are 'on the edge of losing their tempers' all create toxicity. And so, a key point to make here, and one that is similar to our earlier discussion of accountability, is that managers are asked here not only to focus their attention downwards to the conduct of their staff, but also laterally and vertically to their bosses. But more than this it is just as important that consideration is given to the structural and systemic factors that might generate toxic behaviour among colleagues:

> Their [people causing toxicity] actions may in fact be the result of
> systemic organizational forces operating over a prolonged period of time.
> Organizations (...) have the power to erode empathic behavior and to supplant
> it with destructive acts. Zimbardo (2004) in fact argues that the focus on
> individuals acts as a 'smokescreen'.[17]

Micromanagement is another major cause of toxicity. It is based on the belief that quality work will not occur unless it is carefully and at times meticulously supervised. The implication of micromanagement is that workers cannot be trusted to finish a task to time, to a particular standard, or at all. It has been proposed that micromanagers can be psychologically distant, insensitive and imposing (Kim and Yuki, 1995[18]; Pedraja-Rejas et al, 2006[19]).

The 'zero tolerance manager' is equally insensitive and similarly attributes poor performance (in their terms) to individual employee characteristics, such as laziness, incompetence, or a lack of effort (Moss and Sanchez, 2004[20]). This kind of management style can breed what Zukav and Francis (2001[21]) termed 'pleasers', or persons devoid of self-respect whose mindset is formed from hearing others' opinions. Pleasers operate from the premise that the other person is always right. Their intense desire to please is created by fear of not gaining their manager's admiration, not meeting his or her psychological needs (Zukav and Francis, 2001), or potentially losing their status as most favoured sycophant. Pleasers are in a constant state of fear and arousal:

> An individual who needs to please is constantly trying to see how others are
> feeling so that she will know how to be with them. She cannot take their
> requests and communications at face value. She tries to guess what they

are really saying or requesting. This occurs because she herself does not communicate what she is feeling, thinking, or requesting.[22]

Our research work in support of this book revealed a striking number of instances (most of the people we spoke to could recall personal examples of toxicity) of employees experiencing toxicity in work which had engendered some if not all of the following reactions, namely stress, illness, low self-esteem, the desire to leave, suspicion, fear and various coping behaviours. While many of the examples given related to the behaviour of managers this applied also to colleagues, peers and the conduct of people at more junior levels. It goes without saying that this had a damaging effect on the ability to be authentic at work.

Our encouragement here to managers is to leverage the position and power that they have to address concerns such as these quickly, clinically and firmly. This needs to be done not only in relation to individuals perpetrating such behaviour but, as Zimbardo suggests, this needs to be marshalled towards the surrounding power structures and systems that reinforce toxicity.

We end with a metaphor that captures the richness of the task that faces managers, that is the metaphor of a fish tank to further explain the manager's role. We borrow from the work of Dr William Tate at the Institute for Systemic Leadership to articulate this:

> When we peer closely into the fish tank (...) and use our imaginations we see all manner of things. We notice how good swimmers some of the fish are, (...) species whose job is to clear up the mess, (...) those who appear to be stressed out (...) predators, bullies and gangs [and so much more].[23]

Managerial intervention: example 2 – at times of crisis

There are times when we might call upon managers not to invite their people to exercise their Freedom to Operate, not to invite the Freedom to Speak, nor to inspire exploration of a deeper purpose (F2A), but instead to command people to act. A crisis might be one example of this, where the following conditions apply (based on the work of Professor Keith Grint):

- The circumstances are a self-evident crisis.
- There is general uncertainty.
- There is no time or little time for discussion or dissent.
- Coercion is legitimized and necessary in the circumstances for the public good.
- Command seems the most appropriate style.

Of course, it may be that the 'commander' (manager) remains privately uncertain about whether the action is appropriate or whether the situation is indeed a crisis, but such uncertainty will probably not be apparent to the followers of the commander. Examples might include the immediate response to a major train crash, a leak from a nuclear plant, a military attack, a heart attack, an industrial strike, the loss of employment, or a terrorist attack. In situations such as these we look to managers to take decisive action and to place certain factors, such as personal safety, above the freedoms discussed, such as the Freedom to Operate.

In doing this the benefits of a directive form of management during crises can be many and include:

- a speedy response;
- an efficient response;
- a singular form of response; and
- an orderly response.

But, we also invite circumspection in apprehending situations as crises, and we look to managers to develop capabilities and experience that will help them in this work. For example, we can observe that crises might also be constructed in order to legitimate the actions that follow. In fact we might argue, at a fundamental level, that all crises require to be identified as such in order for a crisis management response to follow. A high profile illustration of this might be the 45-minute Weapons of Mass Destruction (WMD) claim made prior to the second war in the Gulf. In this example the action that this then legitimized was on a grand scale and for this reason alone necessitated a clear and present danger. Many would argue that this was not sufficiently demonstrated.

Managerial intervention: example 3 – when individual obligations are not being observed

Earlier, we highlighted six key obligations belonging to workers as they enact the three freedoms (to Operate, to Speak and to Actualize). A reminder of these is shown below:

1 Corporate awareness: the obligation to engage with the corporate messages and priorities of the organization so that freedoms are taken in full awareness of these, eg attendance and participation in formal corporate communication sessions such as 'town hall' meetings.

2 Ethics and values: the obligation to honour the ethics and values of the organization when acting on freedoms.

3 Learning: the obligation to proactively share the success or otherwise of acting on the freedoms.

4 Risk: the obligation to undertake 'de-risking' activity when attempting new and novel approaches, eg committing to making small changes and learning quickly rather than making big changes without first establishing the value of the change.

5 Consequential awareness: the obligation to build understanding (and act on this) of the potential impact of changes and actions arising from freedoms, eg the knock-on effect to other people and roles.

6 Accountability: the obligation to accept accountability for actions that arise from accepting freedoms.

Management interventions in this regard will necessarily take different forms, and this is because different obligations carry different risks. For example, while it is supremely important that learning is generated through the exercise of freedoms, failure to do so can be thought of as in the range of low to medium risk. By contrast, if workers claim the Freedom to Operate, for example, but do so without taking into account whether their actions are ethical or are in line with the organization's values, then the risk will be commensurately higher.

The managerial role in this context is to identify, assess, anticipate and, where appropriate, act on the risks that arise from the conduct of individuals. Styles of intervention may vary. In relation to the obligation to disseminate learning from the freedoms, it would seem more appropriate for managers to adopt a coaching or mentoring role. We might also borrow from the notion found in Behavioural Economics of managers 'nudging' their workers to remain true to their obligations. The particular design of nudges would be for the individual manager to determine, but could in this example involve creating learning report systems that are easy and enjoyable to do. Managers might establish regular learning forums and events. In other situations it might be more appropriate to facilitate more informal learning discussions.

In relation to individuals not honouring the values of the organization we might imagine a swifter response being required. First though, we would want to ensure that the values are well publicized and understood, and that the organization doesn't in fact enact different norms that would effectively undermine the values. We can often see a tension between espoused and lived values and one such example springs to mind. This relates to the UK Members of Parliament expenses scandal of 2009. The UK MP's expenses scandal saw public outrage at the conduct of Members of Parliament in relation to their claims for accommodation, travel, furnishings etc in support of their work.

On 8 May 2009, a UK national newspaper, the *Daily Telegraph*, revealed controversial details regarding the expenses claims of a number of high-profile political figures. This included members of the Prime Minister's Cabinet as well as a number of lesser-known politicians. Initial reports referred to instances such as the Communities Secretary who had claimed approximately £5,000 of public money for furniture for three different properties in one year. Lord Mandelson the Business Secretary had his expenses profiled which included claims for £3,000 to improve his constituency home after he had announced his resignation as an MP, and Margaret Beckett the Secretary for Housing who, over four years, claimed £72,537 for her constituency house despite not having to pay rent or mortgage for the property. At one level these might have seen like fairly minor amounts of money, however as the story developed it was clear that many more MPs had been making similar, sometimes more unusual and increasingly large claims. The police at Scotland Yard were asked in to examine the claims made to determine whether there had been 'wrongdoing'. Many have argued that it had become 'normal' for MPs to seek compensation through expenses arrangements for what they judged to be a low salary for the job.

As the case unfolded more serious criminal proceedings were brought. It was announced on 5 February 2010 that criminal charges would be prosecuted against Labour MPs Elliot Morley, David Chaytor and Jim Devine, and Conservative peer Lord Hanningfield in relation to false accounting. The Crown Prosecution Service announced on 19 May 2010 that Labour MP Eric Illsley would be charged with three counts of false accounting; he was also suspended from the Labour Party. It was revealed Lord Taylor of Warwick, a Conservative peer, had been charged with six counts of false accounting. On 13 October 2010 it was announced that former Labour MP Margaret Moran would also be charged with false accounting, while on 14 October 2010 former Minister of State for Europe and Labour MP Denis MacShane was referred to the police following a complaint from the British National Party, as a consequence of which he was also suspended from the Labour Party. Three Labour Peers were suspended on 18 October 2010 due to their expenses claims: Lord Bhatia was suspended from the House of Lords for eight months and told to repay £27,446; Lord Paul was suspended from the House of Lords for four months and ordered to pay back £41,982 and Baroness Uddin faces a police investigation for alleged fraud for claiming at least £180,000 in expenses by designating an empty flat, and previously an allegedly non-existent property as her main residence. She was suspended from the House of Lords until the end of 2012 and required to repay £125,349. On 3 December 2010 David Chaytor pleaded guilty to charges of false accounting in relation to parliamentary expenses claims and was sentenced to 18 months imprisonment in early 2011.

The behaviour of Members of Parliament is ostensibly underpinned by a set of values that collectively form a code of conduct. There are seven values identified in the code, specifically selflessness, integrity, objectivity, accountability, openness, honesty and leadership. The very first of the 60 recommendations made in the Committee on Standards in Public Life's report in November 2009 was as follows:

> MPs should always act in accordance with the Seven Principles of Public Life. Any future changes to MPs' expenses should be underpinned by the elaboration of those principles set out in the executive summary and repeated in Chapter 3 of this report.[24]

What we witnessed in relation to the MP's expenses scandal was a clear instance of particular behaviours being normalized, eg a lack of openness, honesty, integrity and perhaps even leadership, even though they directly contradict the core values of the organization.

These examples describe the interventions that managers need to make when obligations are not honoured, but it also illustrates the range of approaches that are available, from coaching to tougher interventions, and from nudging to more deeply understanding what norms are at play.

Notes

1 *Administration industrielle et générale – prévoyance organization – commandment, coordination – contrôle*, Paris: Dunod, 1966.
2 Ryde, R (2012) *Never Mind the Bosses: Hastening the death of deference for business success*, Wiley & Sons, p 65.
3 Satyam Sums Up Asian Governance Failings, *Financial Times*, 12 October 2010.
4 BBC timeline, World Health Organisation, European Centre for Disease Prevention and Control.
5 www.gov.uk/government/organisations/behavioural-insights-team
6 www.gov.uk/government/uploads/system/uploads/attachment_data/file/62529/TLA-1906126.pdf
7 www.gov.uk/government/uploads/system/uploads/attachment_data/file/62529/TLA-1906126.pdf

8 www.hapinternational.org/pool/files/accountability,-strategy-and-ingos.pdf, Professor Mark Moore, p 571.

9 www.ksghauser.harvard.edu/PDF_XLS/workingpapers/workingpaper_33.9.pdf, Professor Mark Moore, p 4.

10 http://right2info.org/access-to-information-laws/access-to-information-laws-overview-and-statutory#_ftnref7

11 http://right2info.org/access-to-information-laws/access-to-information-laws-overview-and-statutory#_ftnref7

12 Information Law Lifts Indian Poor, *BBC News*, 14 November 2006, by Mark Dummett.

13 Information Law Lifts Indian Poor, *BBC News*, 14 November 2006, by Mark Dummett.

14 UK organisations paying lip service to whistleblowing, *Public Concern at Work* [online] www.pcaw.org.uk/files/01%20EY%20Research%20Release%20 FINAL.pdf [accessed 29 January 2014].

15 UK organisations paying lip service to whistleblowing, *Public Concern at Work* [online] www.pcaw.org.uk/files/01%20EY%20Research%20Release%20 FINAL.pdf [accessed 29 January 2014].

16 Gilbert, J A, Carr-Ruffino, N, Ivancevich, J M and Konopaske, R (2012) Toxic versus cooperative behaviors at work: The role of organizational culture and leadership in creating community-centered organizations, *International Journal of Leadership Studies*, 7 (1), pp 29–47.

17 www.regent.edu/acad/global/publications/ijls/new/vol7iss1/IJLS_Vol 7, Iss 1,_Gilbert_pp 29–47

18 Kim, H and Yuki, G (1995) Relationships of managerial effectiveness and advancement to self-reported and subordinate-reported leadership behaviors from the multiple-linkage mode, *The Leadership Quarterly*, 6, pp 361–77.

19 Pedraja-Rejas, L, Rodriguez-Ponce, E and Rodriguez-Ponce, J (2006) Leadership styles and effectiveness: A study of small firms in Chile, *Interciencia*, 31, pp 500–504.

20 Moss, S E and Sanchez, J I (2004) Are your employees avoiding you? Managerial strategies for closing the feedback gap, *The Academy of Management Executive*, 18, pp 32–46.

21 Zukav, G and Francis, L (2001) *The Heart of the Soul: Emotional awareness*, Fireside, New York.

22 Zukav, G and Francis, L (2001) *The Heart of the Soul: Emotional awareness*, Fireside, New York, p 174.

23 Managing Leadership from a Systemic Perspective, Dr William Tate, London Metropolitan University: Centre for Progressive Leadership White Paper, 26 November 2012, p 9.

24 'MPs' expenses and allowances – Supporting Parliament, safeguarding the taxpayer' Committee of Standards in Public Life, Twelfth Report, Cm 7724, November 2009.

Beyond the tipping point

09

Look at the world around you. It may seem like an immovable, implacable place. It is not. With the slightest push – in just the right place – it can be tipped.[1]

MALCOLM GLADWELL

So far in this book we have:

- underlined the reasons for making authenticity a priority, and the benefits that arise at the individual and organizational level;

- offered the Freedoms and Authenticity model comprising the Freedom to Operate, the Freedom to Speak and the Freedom to Actualize as important catalysts of change;

- introduced a diagnostic tool at the individual level to help direct attention and effort accordingly; and

- shared our view of a new management task, one that stands as an authenticity-friendly approach and one that we feel better reflects the style of management needed in modern times.

Our intention is that these ideas won't just be adopted by the 'workers', or for that matter just by managers, or just by the leadership, rather we appeal to all groups to embrace these ideas. In the first instance, benefits will be enjoyed by the individuals that do this and this should be enough incentive in itself, but secondly, our organizations will benefit too in ways that will help them survive and thrive in these tough times. With this level of engagement we envisage a powerful momentum towards authenticity in the workplace, and as imagined by Malcolm Gladwell in his publication *The Tipping Point*, we picture a positive virus that will spread and come to shape and define modern organizations. Arguably, there is no other way to make change other than through the actions of individuals who come to influence and inspire others.

But we don't treat the workforce as synonymous with the organization. While in terms of a Venn diagram the two circles cross and there is a considerable overlap between the two domains, organizations can possess a power and an identity that is different from the individuals that make it up. Each can possess a different symbolic value. And legally of course, employees are distinct from the entity itself. They are similar, but not one and the same.

It is therefore important to consider what it is that might need to be in place for an organization to be authentic, that isn't covered by the authenticity that is created at an individual/workforce level. In Chapter 7, in support of the diagnostic, we provided a description represented as an archetype of authenticity at the individual level. Here we offer an organization level archetype to help picture what we are looking for.

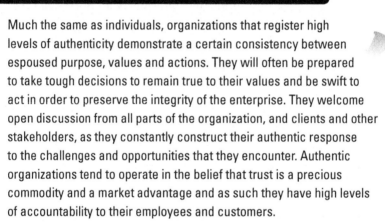

Recognizing authenticity at the organizational level: An archetype

Much the same as individuals, organizations that register high levels of authenticity demonstrate a certain consistency between espoused purpose, values and actions. They will often be prepared to take tough decisions to remain true to their values and be swift to act in order to preserve the integrity of the enterprise. They welcome open discussion from all parts of the organization, and clients and other stakeholders, as they constantly construct their authentic response to the challenges and opportunities that they encounter. Authentic organizations tend to operate in the belief that trust is a precious commodity and a market advantage and as such they have high levels of accountability to their employees and customers.

Recognizing authenticity at an organizational level can be a trickier exercise than seeing it in individuals, so we have set out some of the characteristics that we believe typify authentic organizations that can be used as a point of comparison for anyone wishing to consider their own place of work.

We believe that authentic organizations share clarity around purpose and values. They will have done the hard work to really understand and anatomize the value that they offer to clients, the employee experience and the unique differentiating characteristics of the business. Their values will contain real truths about the organization, rather then simply statements of intent or, worse still, catch all phrases that, while difficult to disagree with, are essentially meaningless. Where employees breach values this will be 'called out' and action taken swiftly. A simply articulated set of values that support the culture and deliver the purpose will run like a golden thread through their decisions and initiatives. Employees will have a deep understanding of this, and in turn this allows for greater autonomy in decision-making.

Authentic organizations do what they say they are going to do. Their deep understanding of the value that they deliver to their clients and their employees informs their decision-making processes. With a clear sense of identity and purpose driving the direction of the organization, the need for spin and circumspection is reduced which builds stakeholder trust. It is worth remembering that, in the age of social media, there is a high probability of being 'found out' if an organization seeks to be less than truthful, and consumers are very likely to take action in such circumstances. This also means that authentic organizations sometimes have to say no, maybe even turn down business, if the request being made of them is incompatible with their purpose and values.

Authentic organizations admit when they are wrong. Even when there is a clear identity and purpose, sometimes organizations don't always get things right. It may be that a product is faulty or the entire strategic plan is off kilter and a complete reinvention is required. In this case, an authentic organization will identify the problem, admit to it and take swift action to remedy the situation. In an environment where all employees, and by extension stakeholders, are listened to and are acting responsibly to de-risk the business, mistakes are less likely to go unchallenged or unrecognized and swift action can be taken to preserve trust.

Organizations that act authentically uphold the value of transparency. It is arguable that an employee cannot fully align their personal values with an organization unless there is transparency of both process and outputs. For example, a committed vegan might struggle to be authentic once they discover that they work in a business that buys factory-farmed meat for its products. Likewise, customers will find it difficult to build trust with an organization that employs secrecy or labyrinthine procedures that may give the impression that it has something to hide. There needs to be a caveat here in that, much the same as with the Freedom to Operate, there will be different extents to which any organization can be transparent. It would not be desirable, for example, for a hospital to breach patient confidentiality. However we invite the same process of challenging the received ideas about transparency and ensuring that it is applied to the fullest extent.

In order to encourage the free flow and diversity of ideas and perspectives, authentic organizations do not build structures of deference. We believe that deference acts against authenticity on any level, as it requires a certain response in relation to position on a hierarchy. Deference is also a symptom of the old Work in the Hand era when workers were dependent upon employers and experts for the tools and knowledge required for production. Since authentic organizations value the unique contribution of employees as individuals, deference falls away, and with it the silencing effect that it has on those further down the grade scale.

As a requirement of integrity of approach, authentic organizations treat their employees and customers similarly. They understand that employees who are valued and able to contribute to their fullest capacity will provide a much more pleasant customer experience. They also know that customers are savvy and will detect any inconsistency between message and experience. However, above and beyond this, we believe that authentic organizations display an adherence to a much older code of practice which is known as The Golden Rule or 'treat others as you would like to be treated yourself'. In this way, we believe that these organizations take on a moral responsibility for their actions that informs and strengthens their commitment to their values.

Typically, authentic organizations demonstrate a high level of trust between colleagues, customers and stakeholders alike. All of the measures of authenticity that we have just outlined work together to build a foundation of trust and credibility. Organizations with a clear purpose, that do what they say they will without hidden agendas or spin, and who admit to making mistakes, are demonstrating credibility that in turn invites trust from all those who connect to it. High trust organizations are attractive to employees and clients who share the same value of authenticity and this in turn can engender loyalty. Office politics and hidden agendas, that can impede the flow of ideas and get in the way of creativity, evaporate in an atmosphere of openness. Creativity and innovation are much more likely in conditions where making an honest mistake is considered part of the creative process and it is well documented that in order to take risk, that is an inevitable part of invention, there must be a proportionate degree of safety for the individual.

As this organizational-level archetype illustrates, while there are differences to observe in relation to the archetype of individual authenticity, there are perhaps many more similarities.

Both place a premium on self-awareness and an appreciation of, and responsiveness to, how they (the employee and the organization) impact on others. We see the importance for both archetypes that is given to understanding and searching to create meaning and value in the work that is done. The ability to openly admit mistakes (rather than conceal them) and by implication to show vulnerability, are authentic qualities of organizations and individuals alike. Near the top of the list for organizations and individuals is the ease with which adult-to-adult communication takes place, where you say what you mean and mean what you say.

There are some areas of difference such as authentic individuals feeling able to freely and naturally talk about what matters to them outside of work. This is not something that a non-sentient entity such as an organization can do other than by virtue of what its people do. Interestingly, though, for individuals we see hierarchy and deference as mechanisms that often stand in the way of authenticity. While organizations operate through deference to differing degrees (and some entirely without it), this could offer up an area of tension.

But the analytical issue in all of this is whether it is sufficient for a workforce (at all levels) to be authentic, in order for an organization itself to be authentic. From a Socratic perspective we might pose this question slightly differently – are there any circumstances in which an entire workforce could be authentic (as defined in this book), for the organization itself to be inauthentic? What we can say for sure is that the more inauthenticity we see enacted around us at work, the more likely it is that the organization itself will follow suit. The more people, for example, that ride roughshod over the values, the greater the probability that the organization will be experienced as inauthentic. The more people that are unable to speak truth unto power, the more that the organization will remain unchecked in its use of power, and we have seen this story play out many times before. The more people that hide their mistakes and act defensively, the more likely that their organization will be judged as inauthentic and treated with suspicion. So our position is yes, having authentic employees goes a long way to making authentic organizations. And we would suggest that an authentic workforce takes the organization the single greatest distance towards authenticity.

But we might conceive of the effects of particular individuals or groups that stand outside the organization that might have an undue influence on its ability to be authentic. Sitting in this cluster of influencers might be shareholders, non-executive directors, legal entities, government, the media, competitors and perhaps even clients and customers. And while we are not suggesting that all of these influencers will routinely challenge an organization's authenticity, we can conceive of times when this might be the case. For example, supermarket chains committed to ethical sourcing might feel their values, and therefore their authenticity, coming under pressure as customers press them for ever lower prices. Shareholders looking for a company to deliver a return on their investment may push the organization away from its core obligations, perhaps tolerating savings and cost reductions on important health and safety commitments.

We believe that most of what needs to be done is tackled at the employee level through the adoption of authenticity and the Freedoms Model. But there are some additional nudges that will help to push the organization in the right direction, at times helping to get it 'over the line' on authenticity, and these are set out in Table 9.1.

We end by reiterating (from Chapter 1) a familiar tale, viewed through a lens of authenticity:

> There once was a shepherd boy who was bored as he sat on the hillside watching the village sheep. To amuse himself he took a great breath and sang out, 'Wolf! Wolf! The wolf is chasing the sheep!' The villagers came running up the hill to help the boy drive the wolf away. But when they arrived at the top of the hill, they found no wolf. The boy laughed at the sight of their angry faces. 'Don't cry "wolf", shepherd boy,' said the villagers, 'When there's no wolf!' They went grumbling back down the hill.
>
> Later, the boy sang out again, 'Wolf! Wolf! The wolf is chasing the sheep!' To his naughty delight, he watched the villagers run up the hill to help him drive the wolf away. When the villagers saw no wolf they sternly said, 'Save your frightened song for when there is really something wrong! Don't cry "wolf" when there is no wolf!'
>
> But the boy just grinned and watched them go grumbling down the hill once more. Later, he saw a real wolf prowling about his flock. Alarmed, he leapt to his feet and sang out as loudly as he could, 'Wolf! Wolf!' But the villagers thought he was trying to fool them again, and so they didn't come.
>
> At sunset, everyone wondered why the shepherd boy hadn't returned to the village with their sheep. They went up the hill to find the boy. They found him weeping. 'There really was a wolf here! The flock has scattered! I cried out, "Wolf!" Why didn't you come?' The old man attempted to comfort the boy, as his blood boiled within.

Continues on p 189

TABLE 9.1 Seven additional nudges to be adopted at the organizational level to create authentic organizations

Additional steps to authenticity at the organizational level	Explanation
1 **Publicly declare what the organization stands for (and will not stand for)**	Declaring what the organization stands for might occur in a number of ways – through the brand, the organization's vision, its credo and so on. But this needs to be genuinely meant and be the result of ongoing deep analysis about what the organization cares about (eg sourcing, quality standards, convenience etc). A superficial process will not do and is too often the first port of call for many organizations. This enables customers to know what to expect, potential employees to know if they wish to join, commentators and analysts to judge organizational performance and so on. Importantly though, many companies leave out what they are not prepared to accept, and this should be seen as just as important. One example relates to the Coca Cola company. We might conjecture during the 2014 Winter Olympics in Sochi, Russia, that the main sponsor Coca Cola were as opposed to the anti-gay laws in Russia at the time as many others were, and yet this is not something they had taken a position on prior to or during their sponsorship of the games. This omission no doubt left customers and stakeholders dissatisfied and unclear on what Coca Cola is prepared to stand against. At best such declarations are genuine and deeply felt, and they also articulate what the organization will not allow, at worst there is either silence from the organization or they offer platitudes.

(continued)

TABLE 9.1 Seven additional nudges to be adopted at the organizational level to create authentic organizations (*continued*)

	Additional steps to authenticity at the organizational level	Explanation
2	**Proactively engage in real, two-way, adult-to-adult dialogue with all that are interested**	This kind of dialogue with stakeholders, clients, customers etc, might be to share the narrative or explain the organization's position but equally it is about creating channels for adult-to-adult communications. And organizations that are respectful of their clients and the community will be serious about establishing multiple means of dialogue. They will be responsive to conversation and comment from outside the organization, and will not ignore 'the elephant in the room'. Good examples of this include First Direct, the online banking provider, who make a virtue out of sharing online all compliments and complaints without editing or suppressing contributions. What you see is what they said and this builds trust and demonstrates authenticity.
3	**Turn the organization into a 'glass house' (highly transparent)**	In this context we see organizations making it a priority to proactively make transparent their performance, results, conduct, partnerships, suppliers etc. For larger organizations it is particularly important that they are prepared to make visible this web of relationships. There is something too that might be borrowed and adapted here from the public sectors in terms of freedom of information processes and proactive declarations. Organizations owe it to their clients and stakeholders to make them aware of how their contribution (money, time, knowledge) is being put to use. And the organization should make it easy, and ideally 'effortless', for people to find this out.

(continued)

TABLE 9.1 Seven additional nudges to be adopted at the organizational level to create authentic organizations (*continued*)

	Additional steps to authenticity at the organizational level	Explanation
4	**Humanize the points of interaction between organization and clients, customers, enquirers etc**	Increasingly we see companies engaging with customers through mechanized systems such as voice-activated customer service phone services (IVR), but also through remote/face-to-face human interactions that follow tightly scripted processes. The famous TV show *Little Britain* with the catch line 'Computer says no!' illustrates this perfectly in that despite dealing with a human operator it feels mechanistic and unresponsive. These and other approaches to engagement have a de-humanizing effect on clients and stakeholders and typically undermine what might otherwise be an authentic relationship. We also see the establishment of websites not as a means of building relationships but very often as a means of building a wall between enquirers and the organization. Even in the case of online businesses where most interactions are without human interaction, customers still want to feel connected to, understood by, and involved in a trusting relationship, so, for example, with return online visits individuals should be recognized (as humans that have seen each other before), their experiences shouldn't be wiped out and the relationship knocked back down to where it first started.
5	**Follow the organization's influence as far as it goes and assess the impact against its standards**	Organizations small and large have far-reaching influence; from the entities that supply to them, the communities that they affect, the customers that they satisfy, the resources they make use of, the taxes they pay and so on. Authentic organizations care about their conduct in each of these domains and in feeling a sense of

(*continued*)

TABLE 9.1 Seven additional nudges to be adopted at the organizational level to create authentic organizations (*continued*)

Additional steps to authenticity at the organizational level	Explanation
	responsibility will map their influence onto them and ensure that their principles are carried through in practice.
6 **Admit to, and share learning from, mistakes**	Good and bad companies alike make mistakes. There is a certain inevitability to this, not least because of the complexity of the modern operating environment and the risks that need to be taken. The authenticity test though is how those mistakes are handled when they arise: are they brushed under the carpet, are they played down, are they only revealed when compelled to be, are they deliberately revealed at a time when other bigger news items will cause them to be overlooked? Authentic organizations will not find themselves answering 'yes' to any of these questions.
7 **Don't change the deal (with customers or employees) and expect no one to notice**	Change is the new constant, and no one (customers, employees, stakeholders etc) would expect organizations to remain static. But people invest in organizations in differing ways based on their offer, their principles, their brand and so on, and should these change then the organization has an obligation to explain this and to respect the reaction that might arise. Take, for example, the merger between telecommunications giants Orange and EE. Prior to the merger, Orange won over many customers as a direct result of their hip, youthful and irreverent brand identity, and customers were invited to accept this not simply as a shallow marketing ploy but something that was meant. However, as a result of the merger the brand lost its

(continued)

TABLE 9.1 Seven additional nudges to be adopted at the organizational level to create authentic organizations (*continued*)

Additional steps to authenticity at the organizational level	Explanation
	'edge' but nevertheless still sought to retain its clients on the same basis as before. And so while authenticity should not prohibit change, people will experience an organization as inauthentic if it fails to provide a meaningful and respectful narrative to its stakeholders.

To recap, there is one winner to the story of the boy and the wolf, and two losers:

- The winner is of course the wolf that got a handsome meal in the process. We might think of the wolf as the competition. Interestingly, the wolf didn't need to change anything about the way it conducted its business, the wolf just carried on as usual and took the advantage that the boy unwittingly provided.

- The first loser is of course the boy, who as an employee is unlikely to be trusted with the role of Shepherd again. His dismissal papers are probably in the post.

- But the second loser is the townspeople (the organization), and all of them, as they collectively relied on the boy in protecting their food supply that now sits in the belly of the competition.

Our moral of this tale is that authenticity between colleagues and across all levels of the system is of first order importance. Most of this book is written on the premise that employees and culture comes first in constructing authenticity and with it comes the benefits discussed, including trust, responsibility, accountability and engagement – all of which were absent in the tale of the boy and the wolf. This chapter offers some strategies for adjusting authenticity at the organizational level, but we are clear that with authentic people, we create authentic organizations.

Note

1 Gladwell, M (2002) *The Tipping Point: How little things can make a big difference*, Abacus, p 259.

INDEX

Note: Page numbers in *italics* indicate figures or tables.

CPSIA information can be obtained at www.ICGtesting.com
Printed in the USA
BVOW06s1142280116

434619BV00014B/38/P